Real World Colouring Book

For Advanced Users & Adults

50 Images

Created From Real Life Photos For You To Colour As You Please.

ISBN 978-0-359-93592-5
90000
9 780359 935925

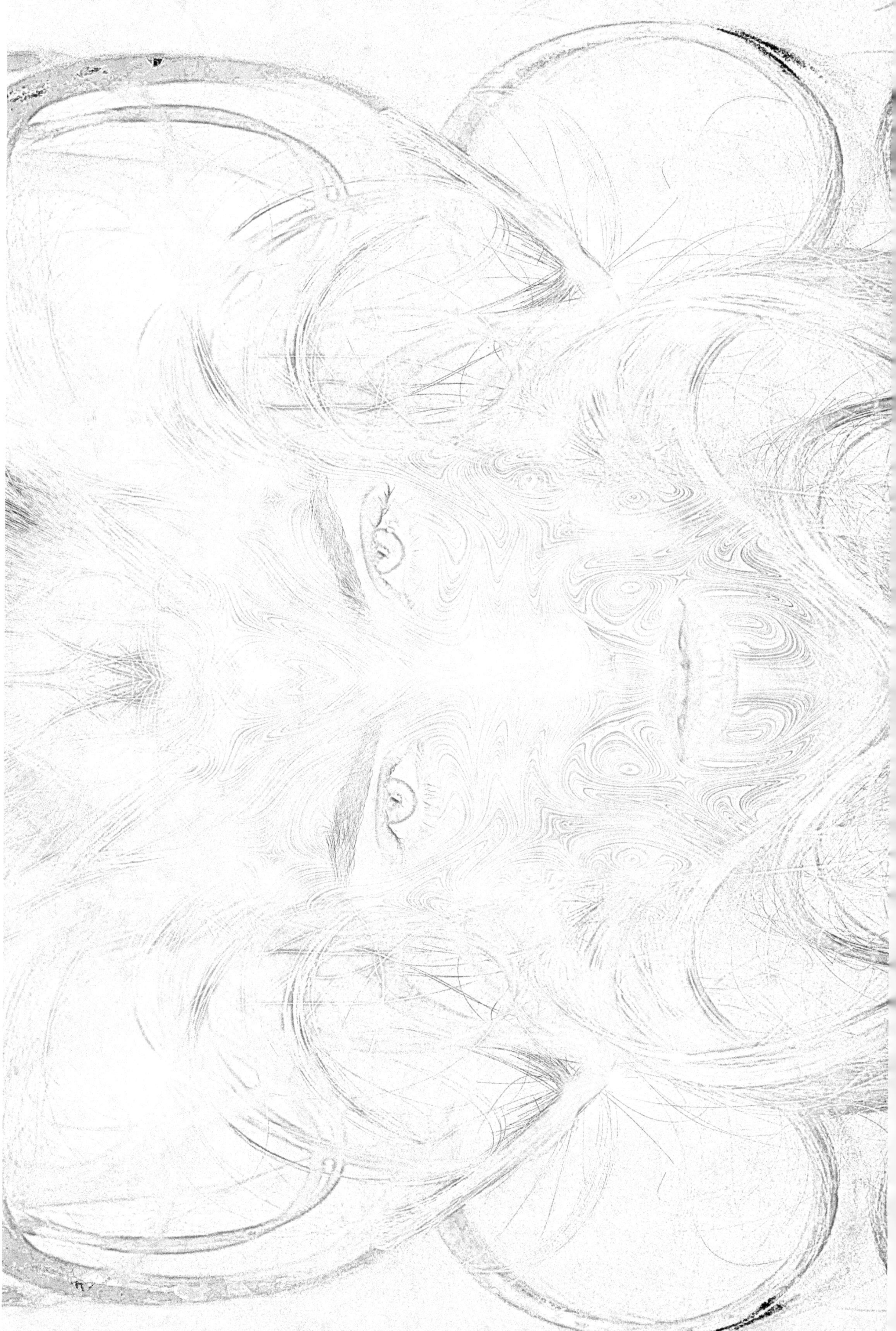

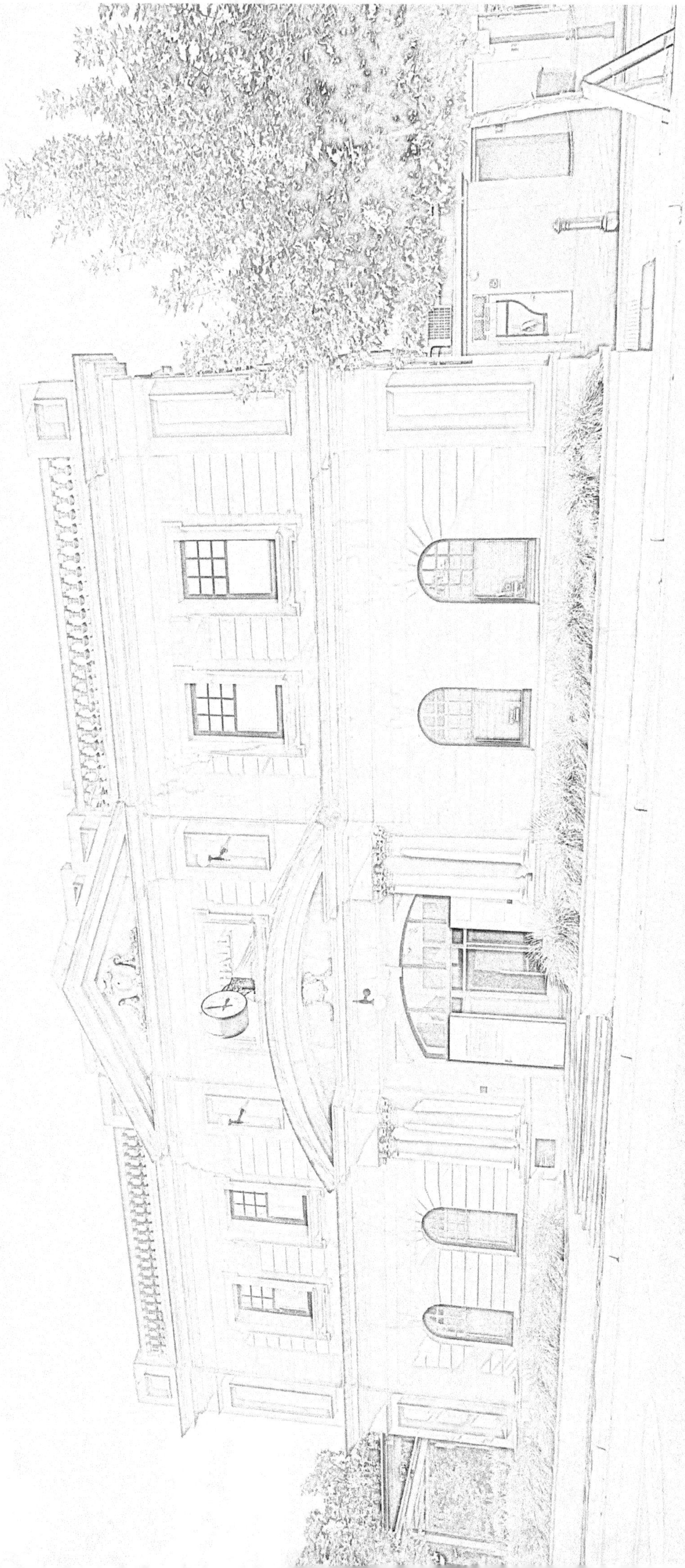

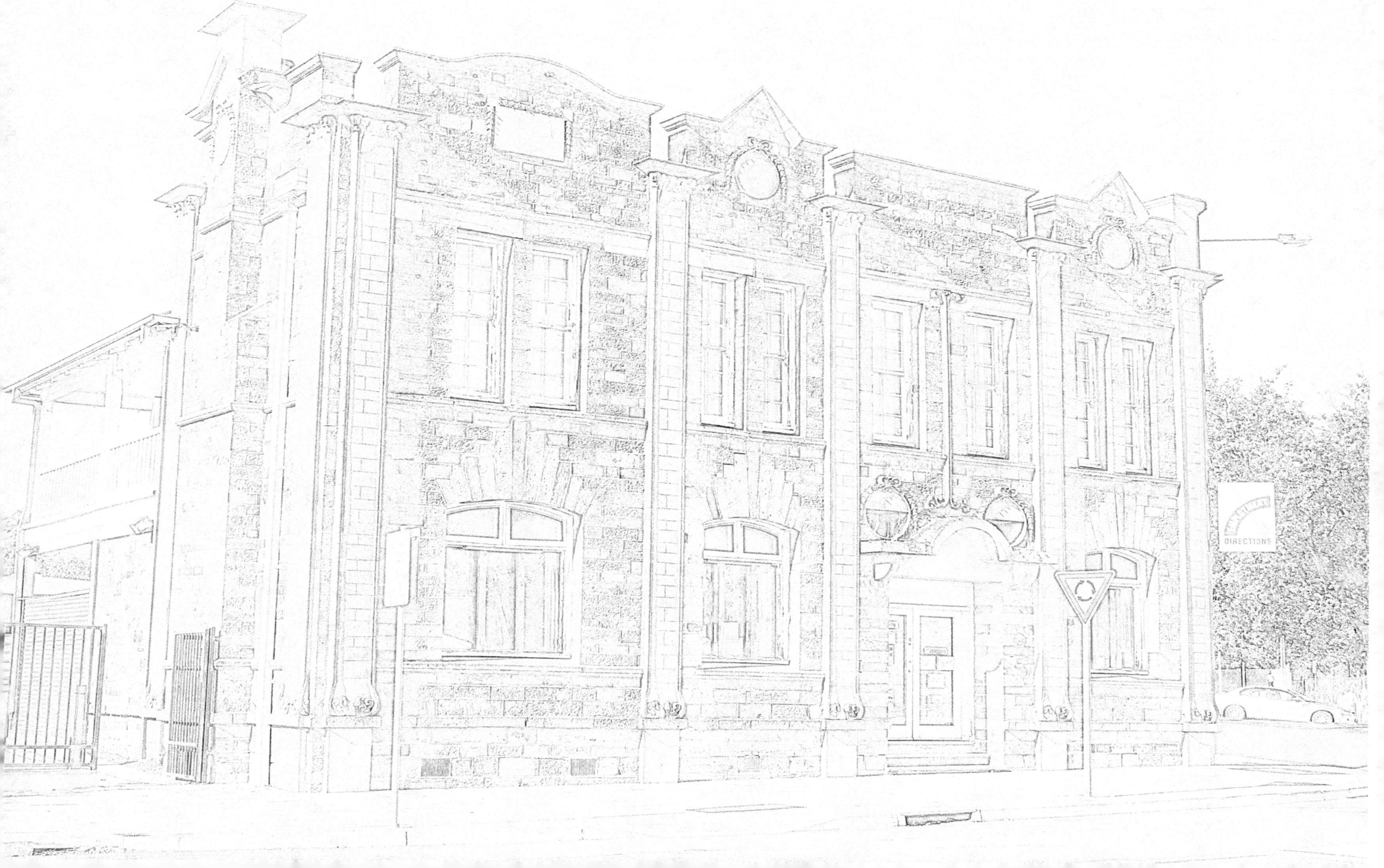
DIRECTIONS

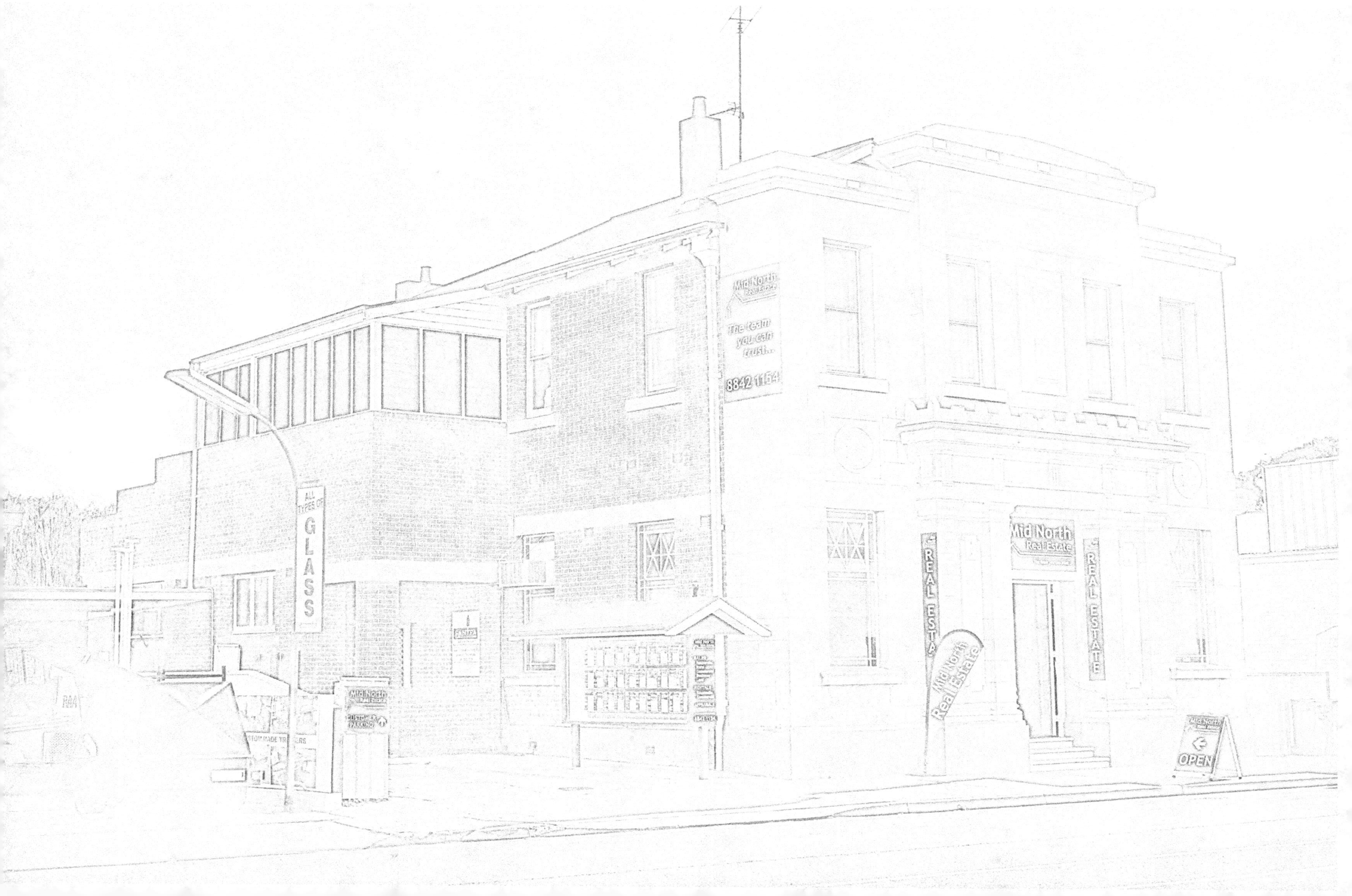

Mid North Real Estate
The team you can trust...
8842 1154
ALL TYPES OF
GLASS
Mid North Real Estate
CUSTOMER PARKING
Mid North Real Estate
REAL ESTATE
REAL ESTATE
Mid North Real Estate
OPEN

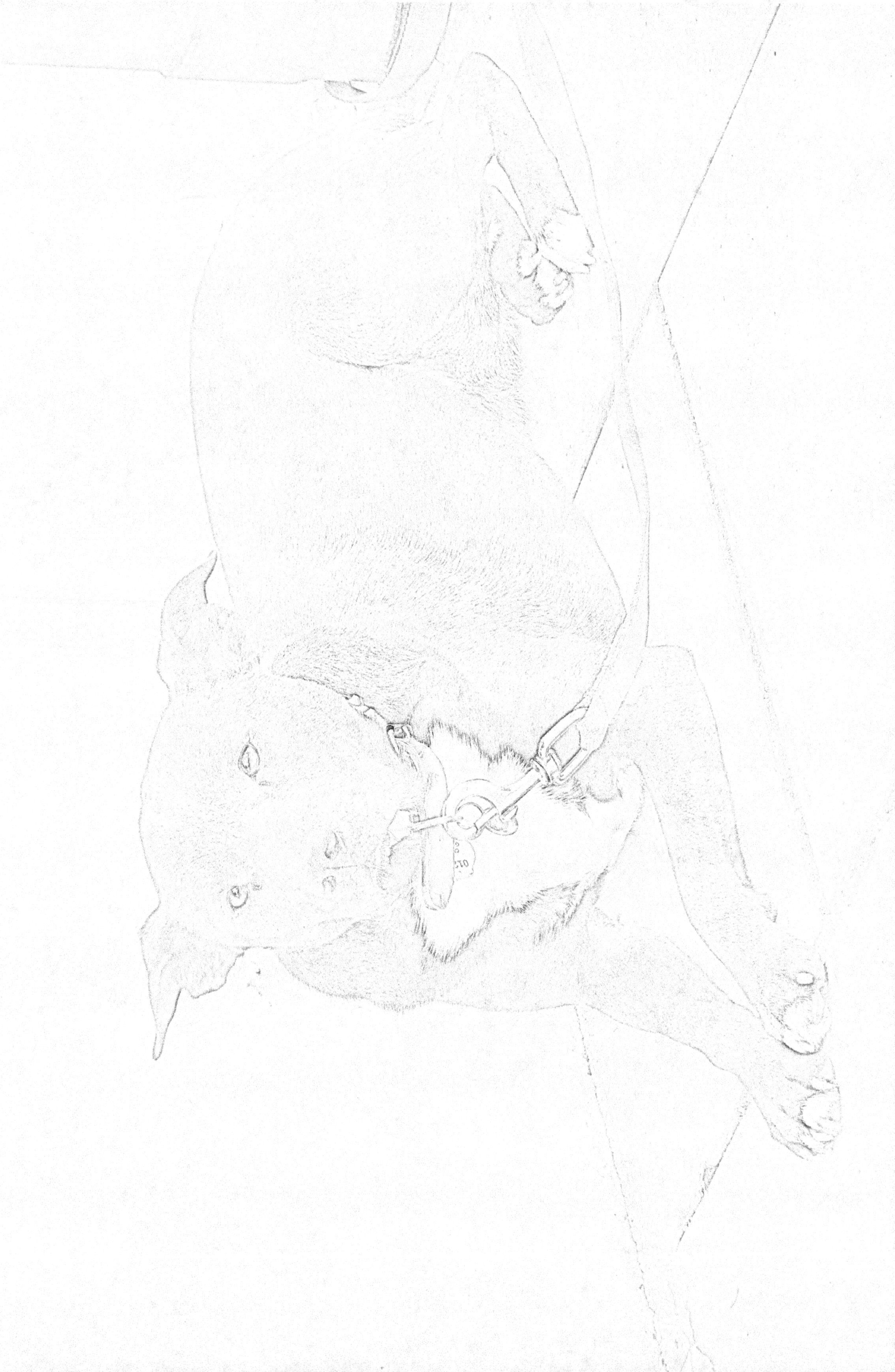

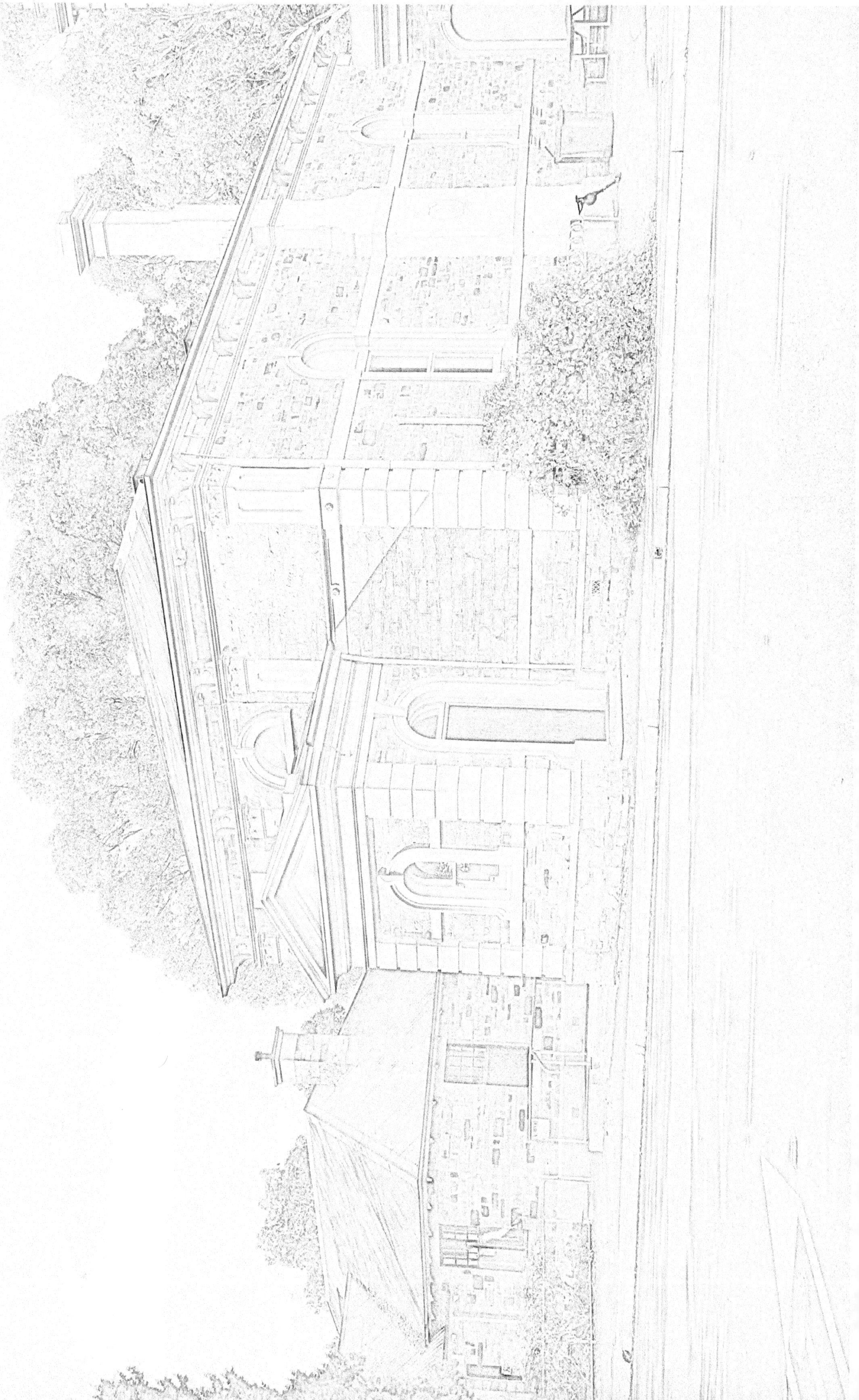

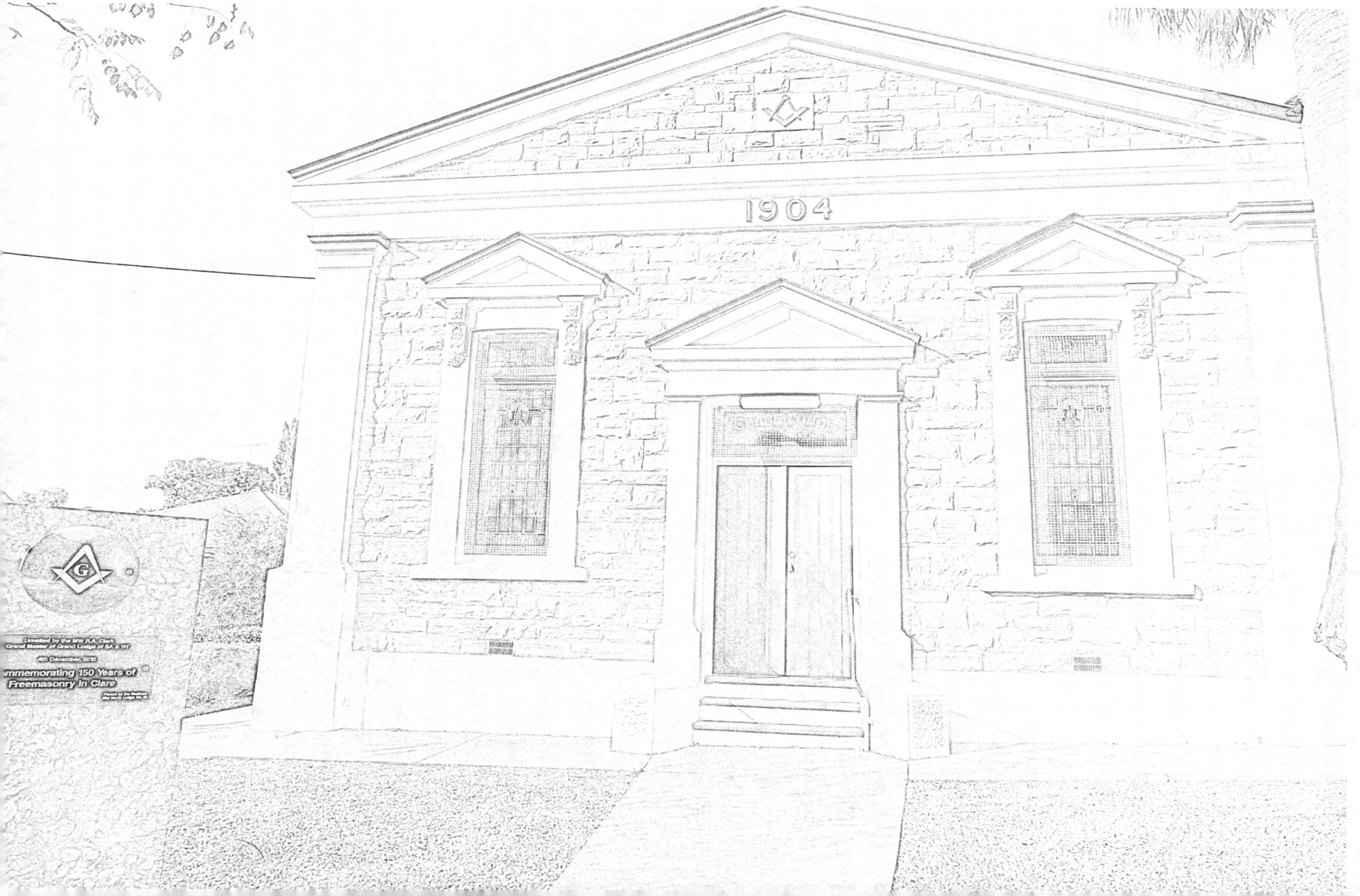
1904
4th December, 2010
mmemorating 150 Years of
Freemasonry In Clare

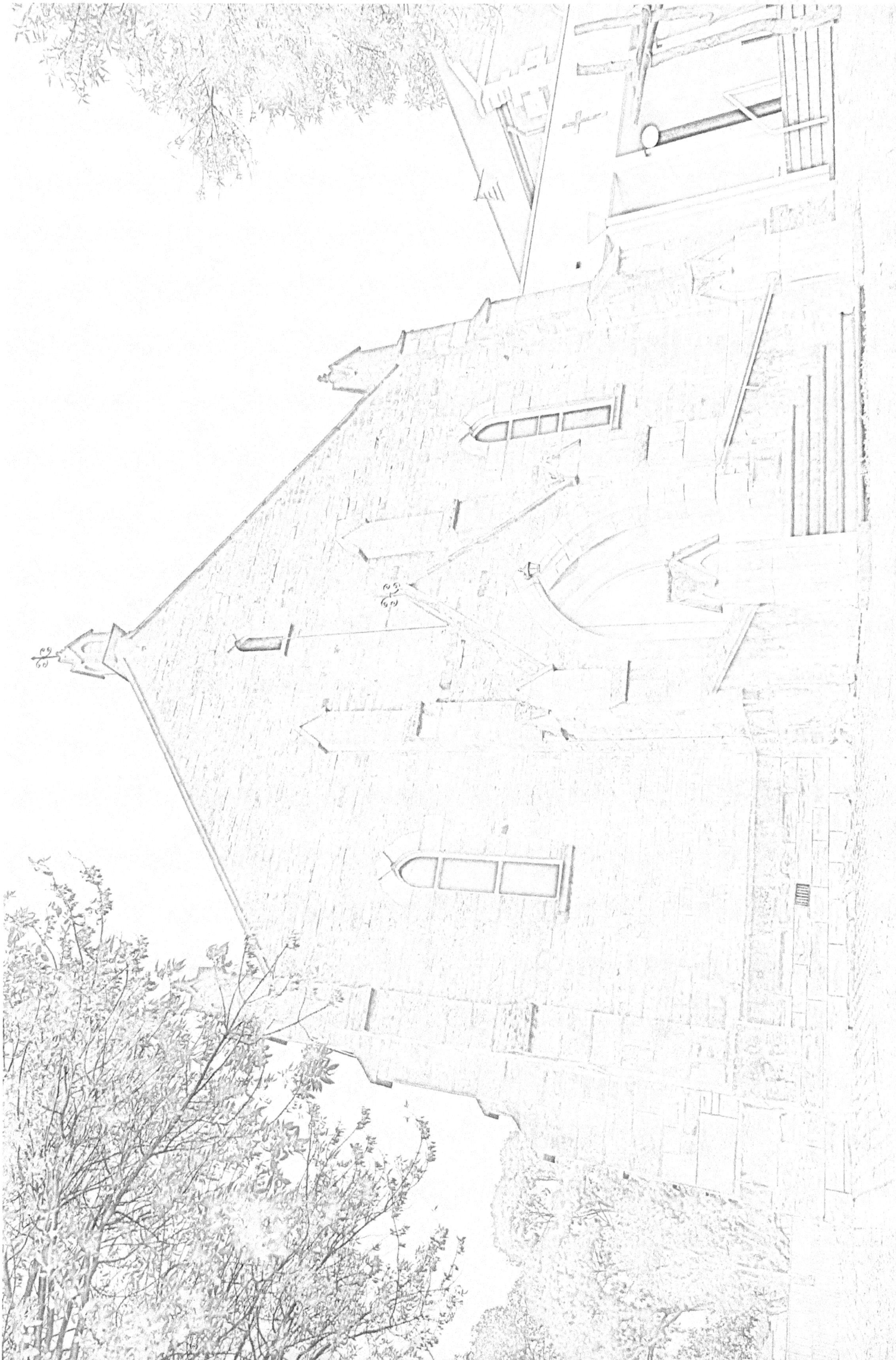

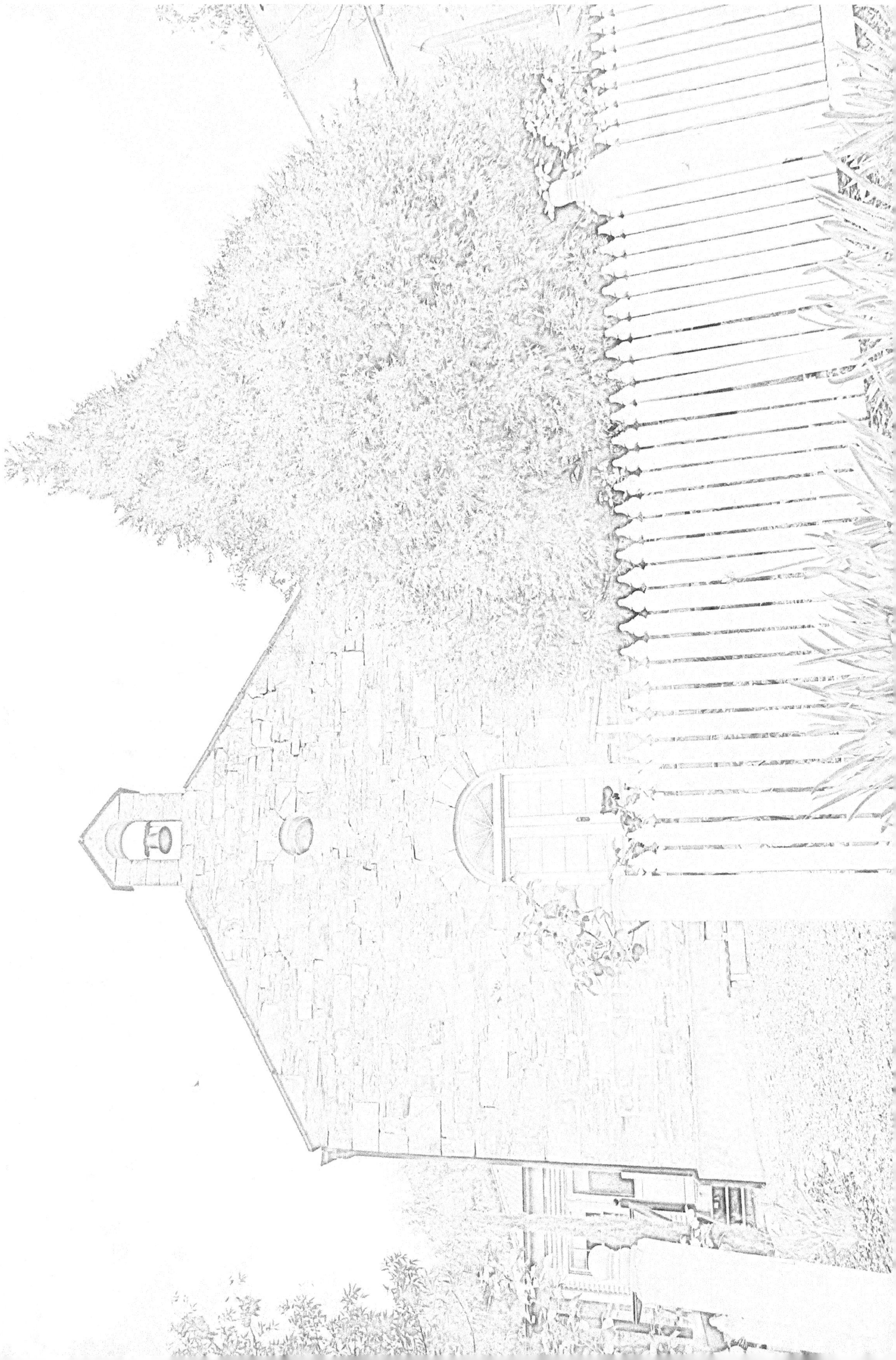

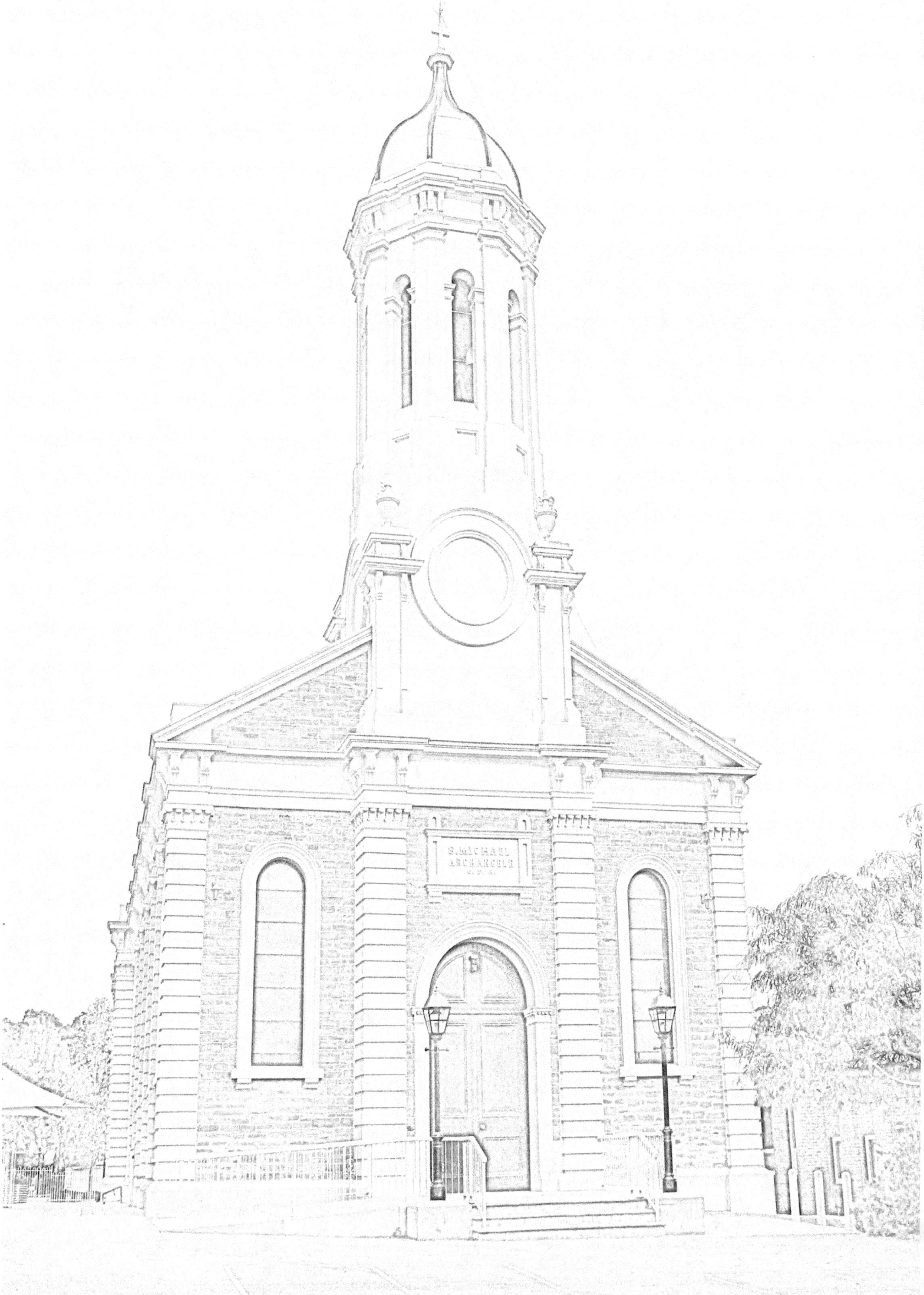
S.MICHAEL
ARCHANGELO

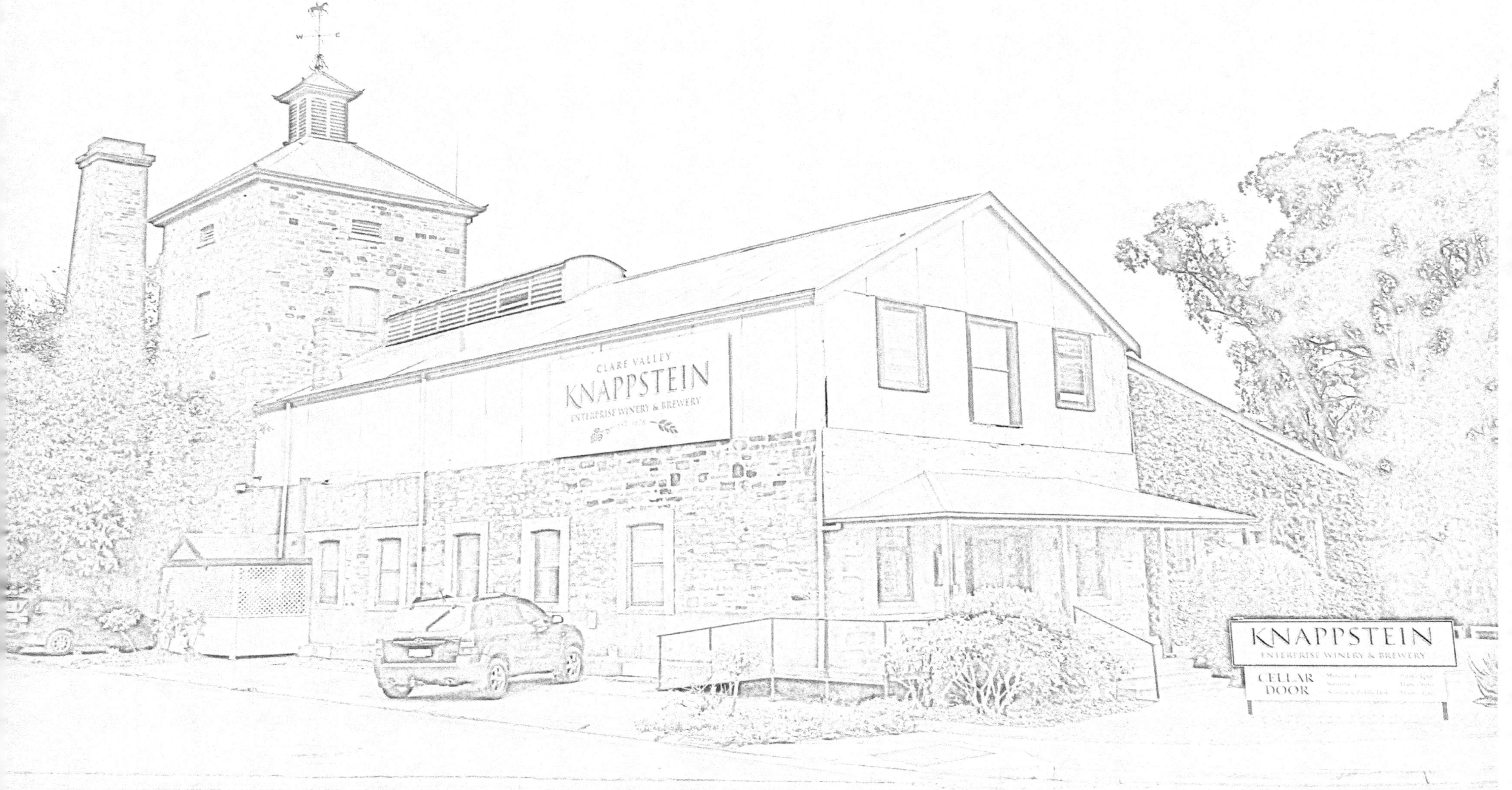
CLARE VALLEY
KNAPPSTEIN
ENTERPRISE WINERY & BREWERY
KNAPPSTEIN
ENTERPRISE WINERY & BREWERY
CELLAR
DOOR

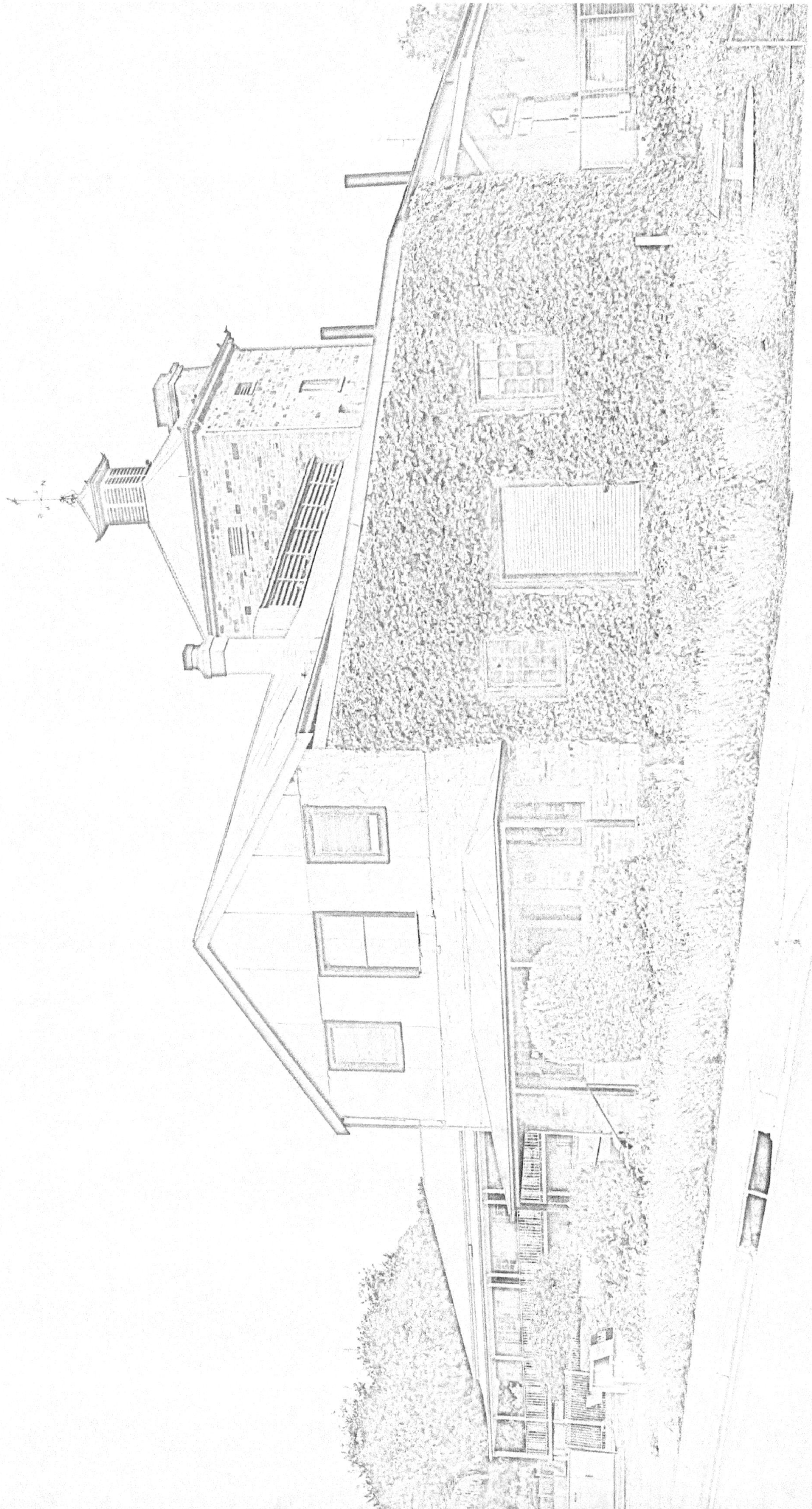

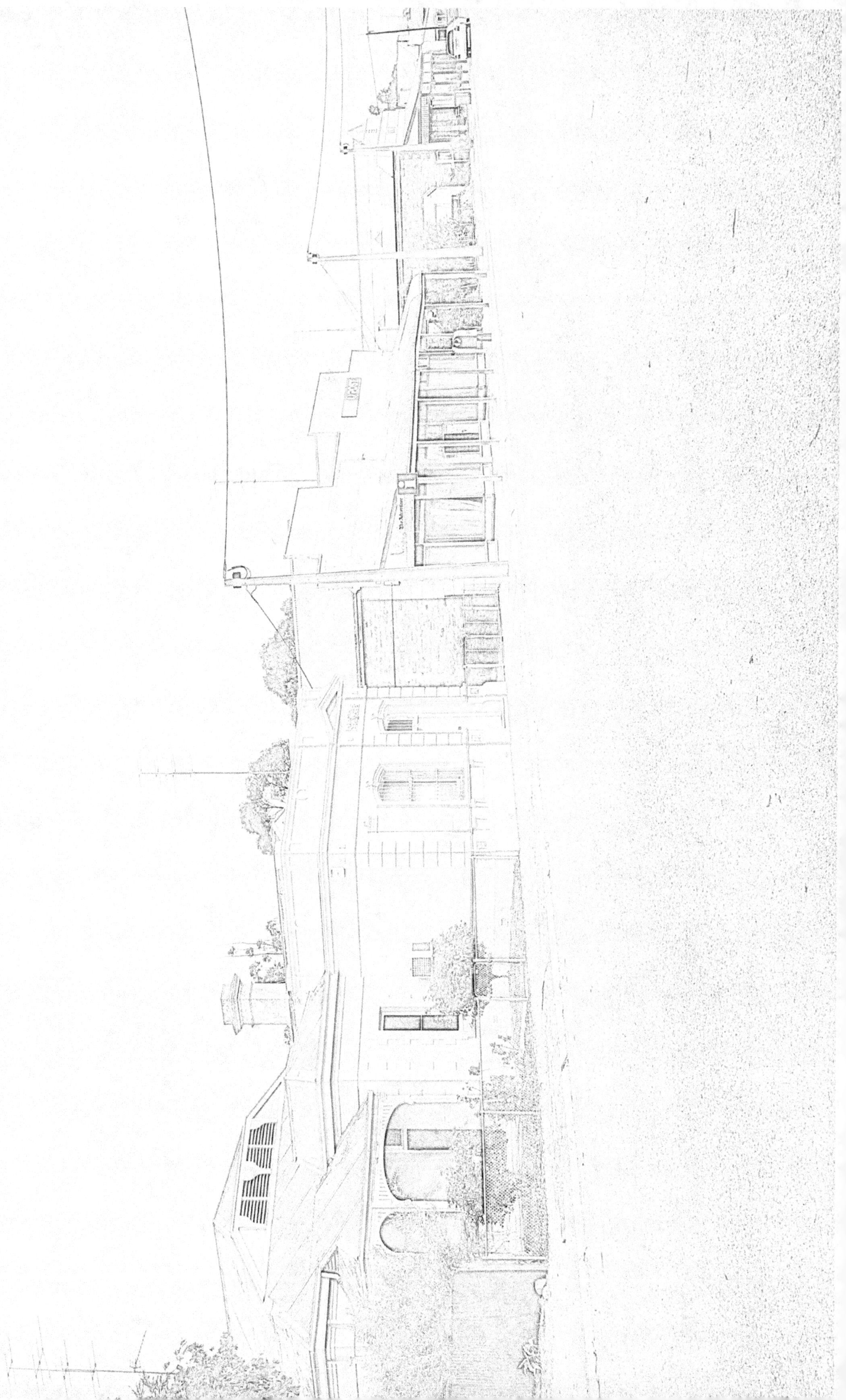

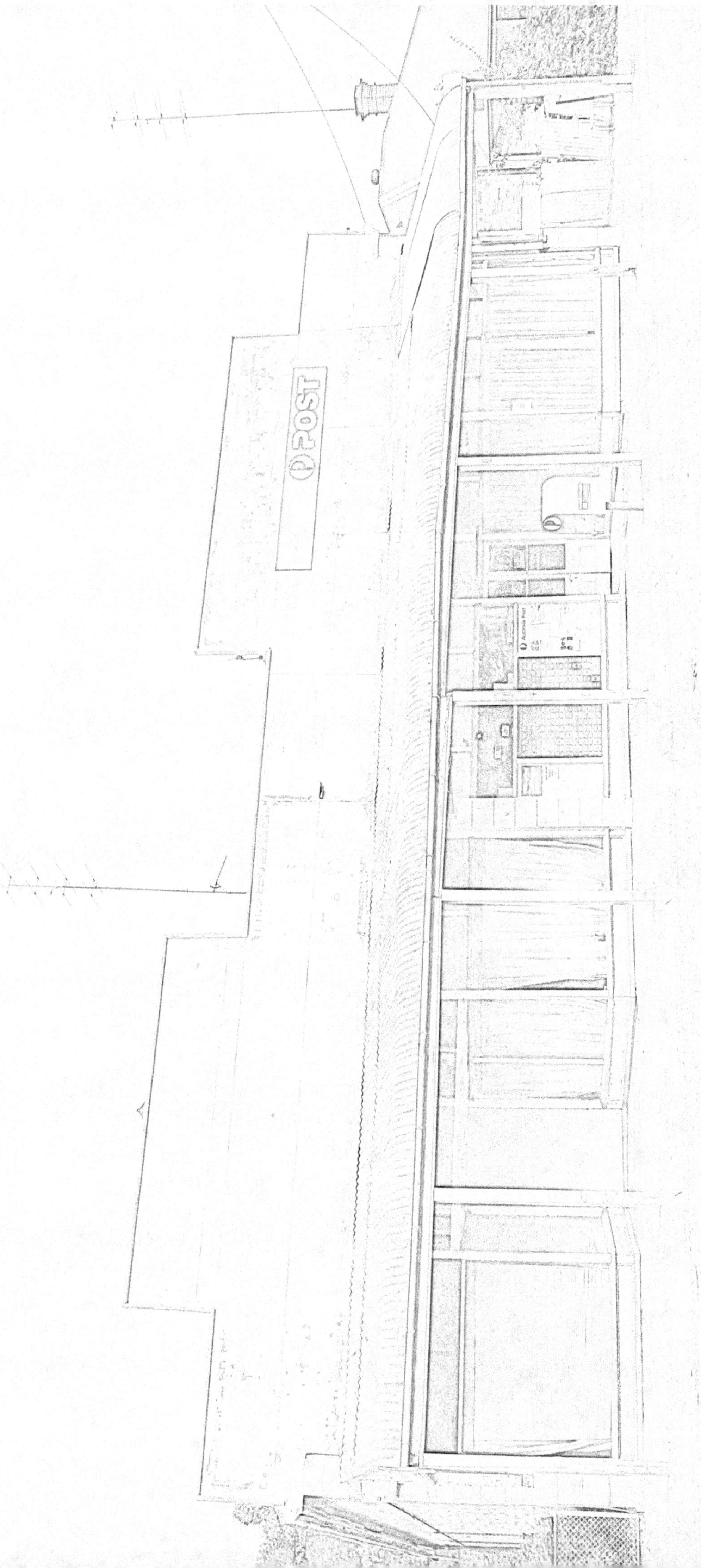
POST

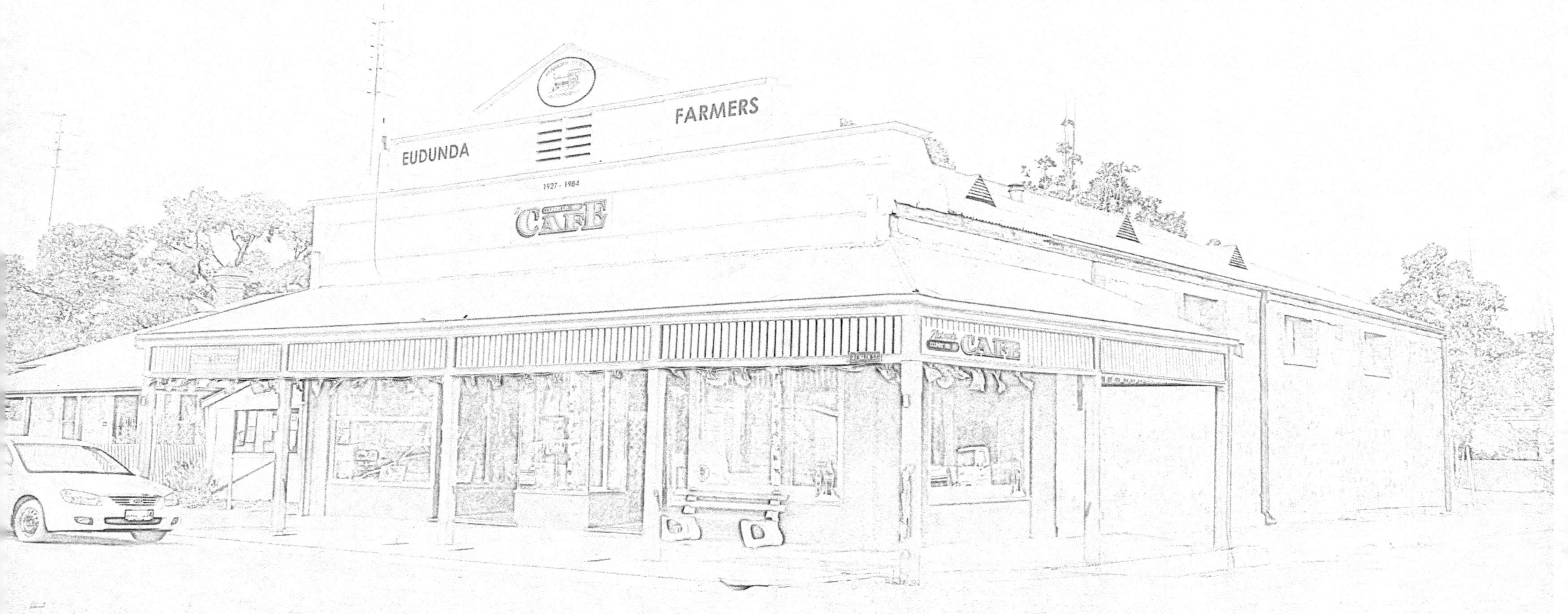
EUDUNDA
FARMERS
1927 - 1984
CAFE
CAFE

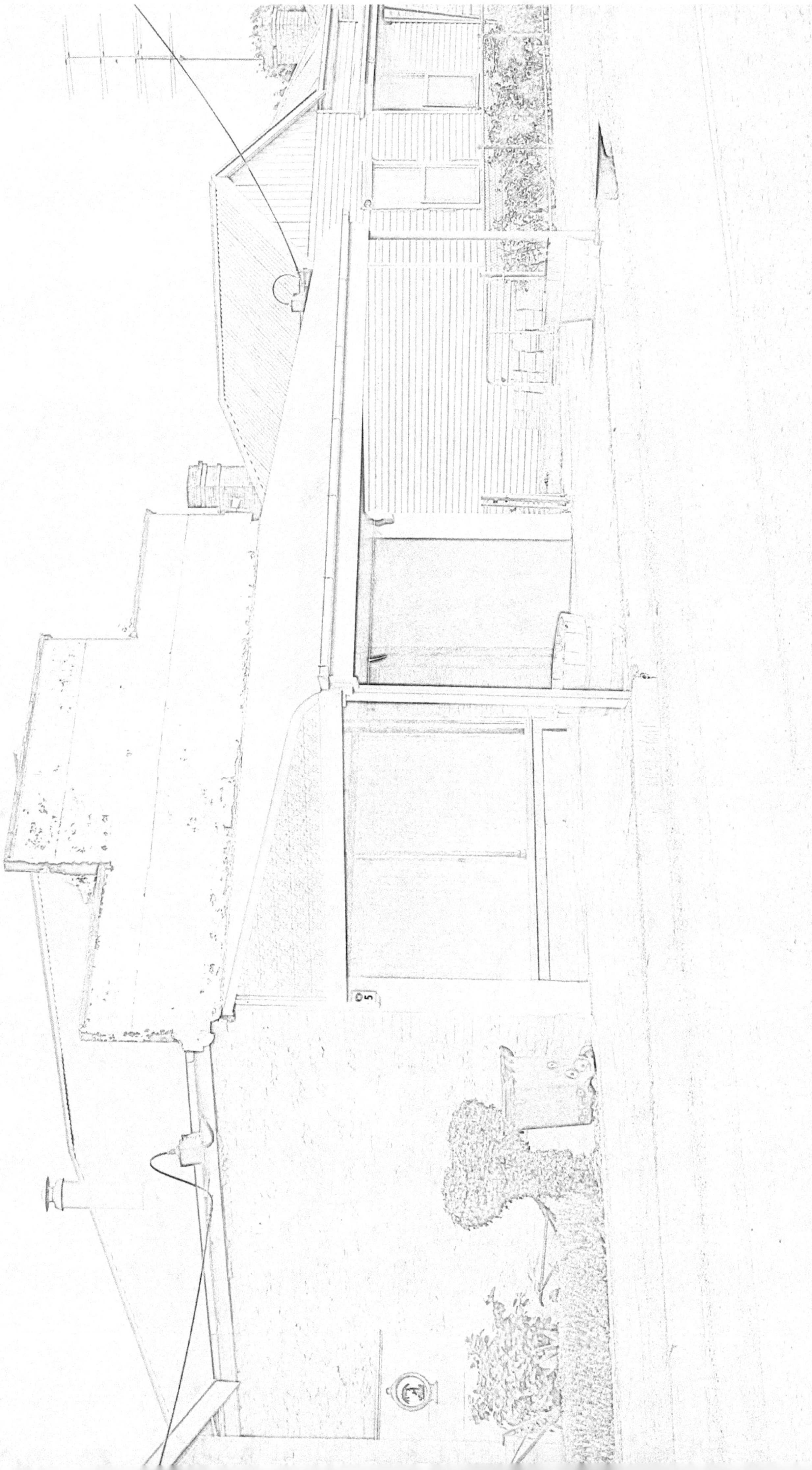

SSS
LP Gas
refills here
Origin
FORD McCARTHY & ASSOCIATES
PUBLIC ACCOUNTANTS
TAXATION CONSULTANTS
VICTA
SALES, SPARES & SERVICE
RAA

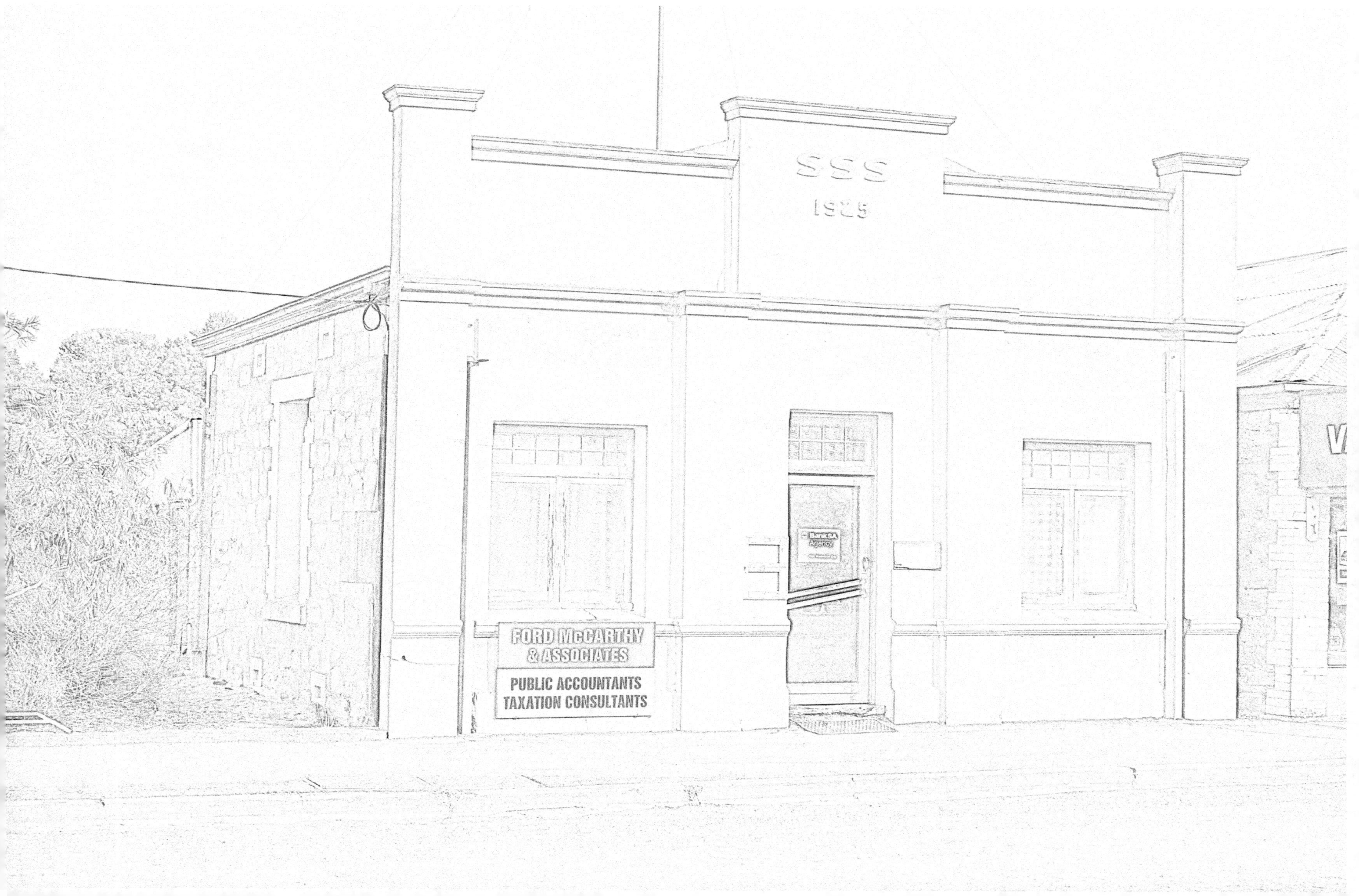
SSS
1925
FORD McCARTHY
& ASSOCIATES
PUBLIC ACCOUNTANTS
TAXATION CONSULTANTS

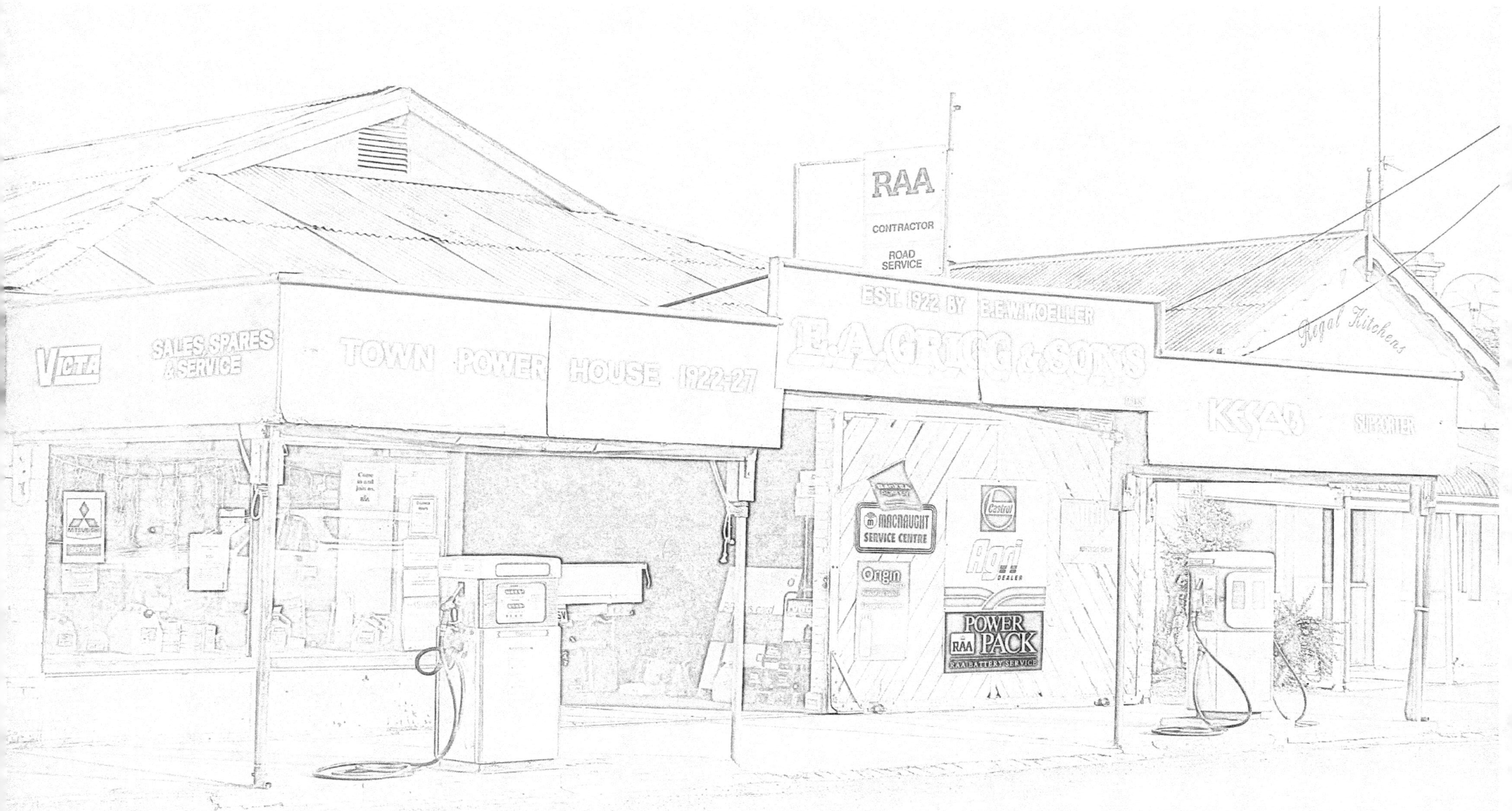

RAA
CONTRACTOR
ROAD SERVICE
VICTA
SALES SPARES & SERVICE
TOWN POWER HOUSE 1922-27
EST. 1922 BY E.E.W. MOELLER
E.A. GRIGG & SONS
Regal Kitchens
KESAB
SUPPORTER
MITSUBISHI
Come in and join us.
MACNAUGHT SERVICE CENTRE
Castrol
Agri DEALER
Origin
POWER PACK
RAA
RAA BATTERY SERVICE

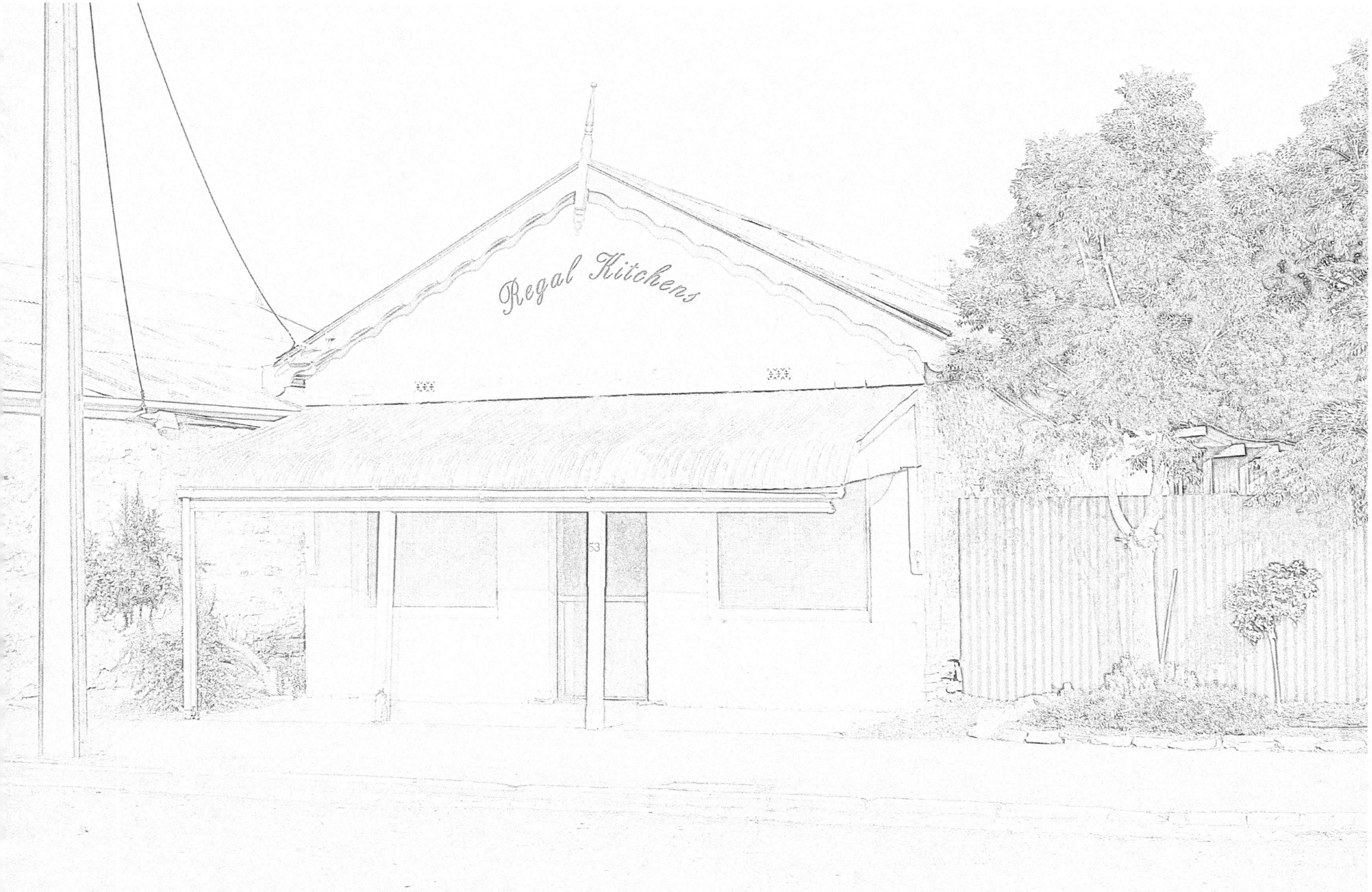
Regal Kitchens
53

BP
Distributor
Supplied

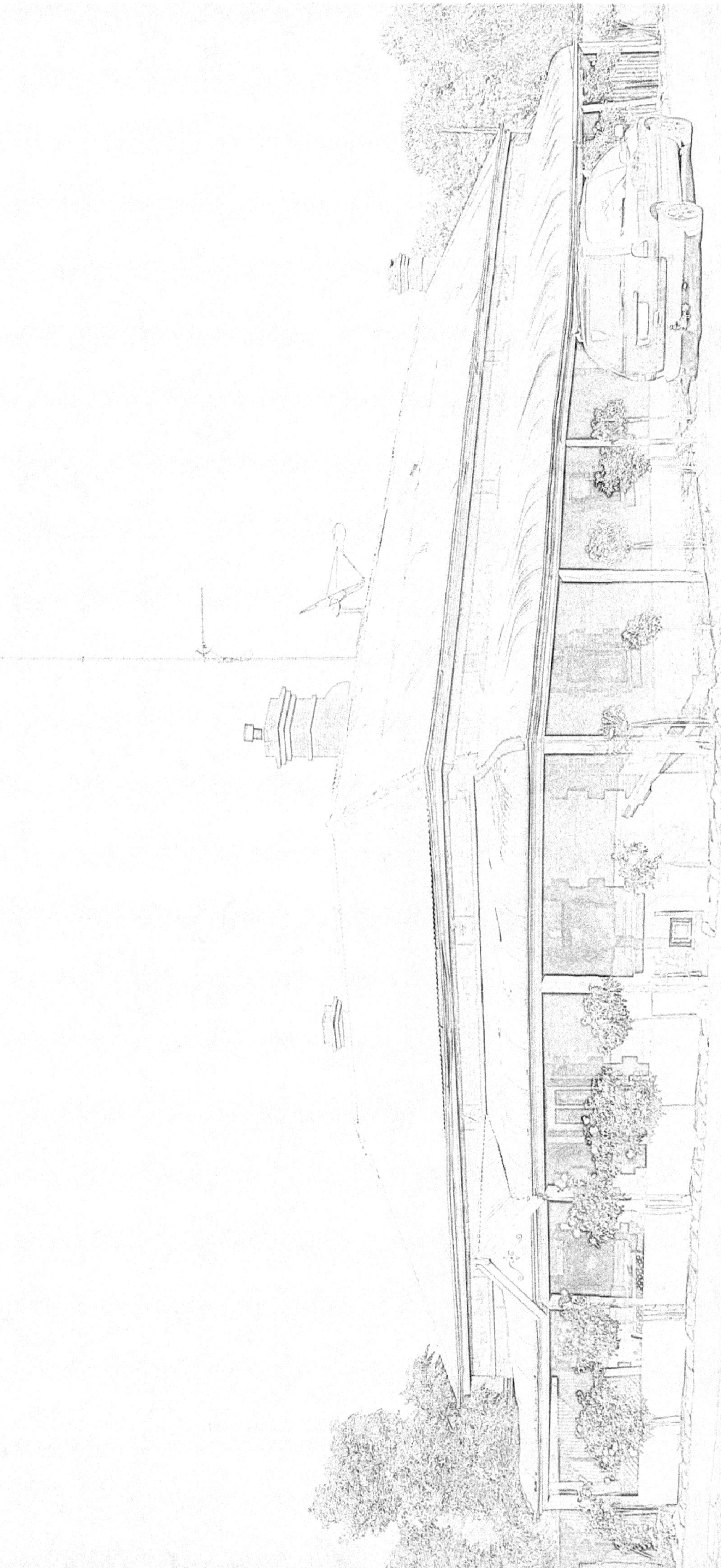

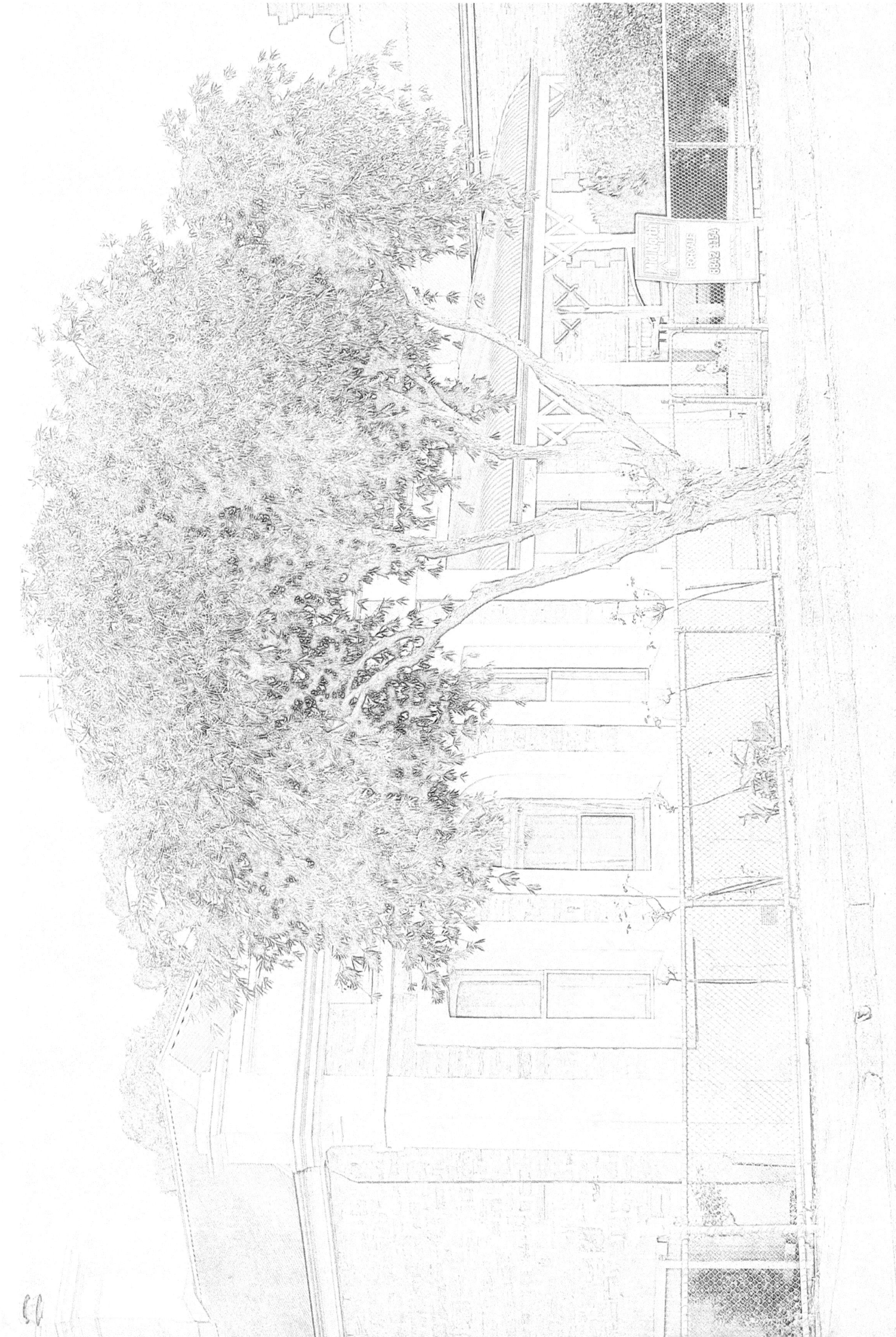

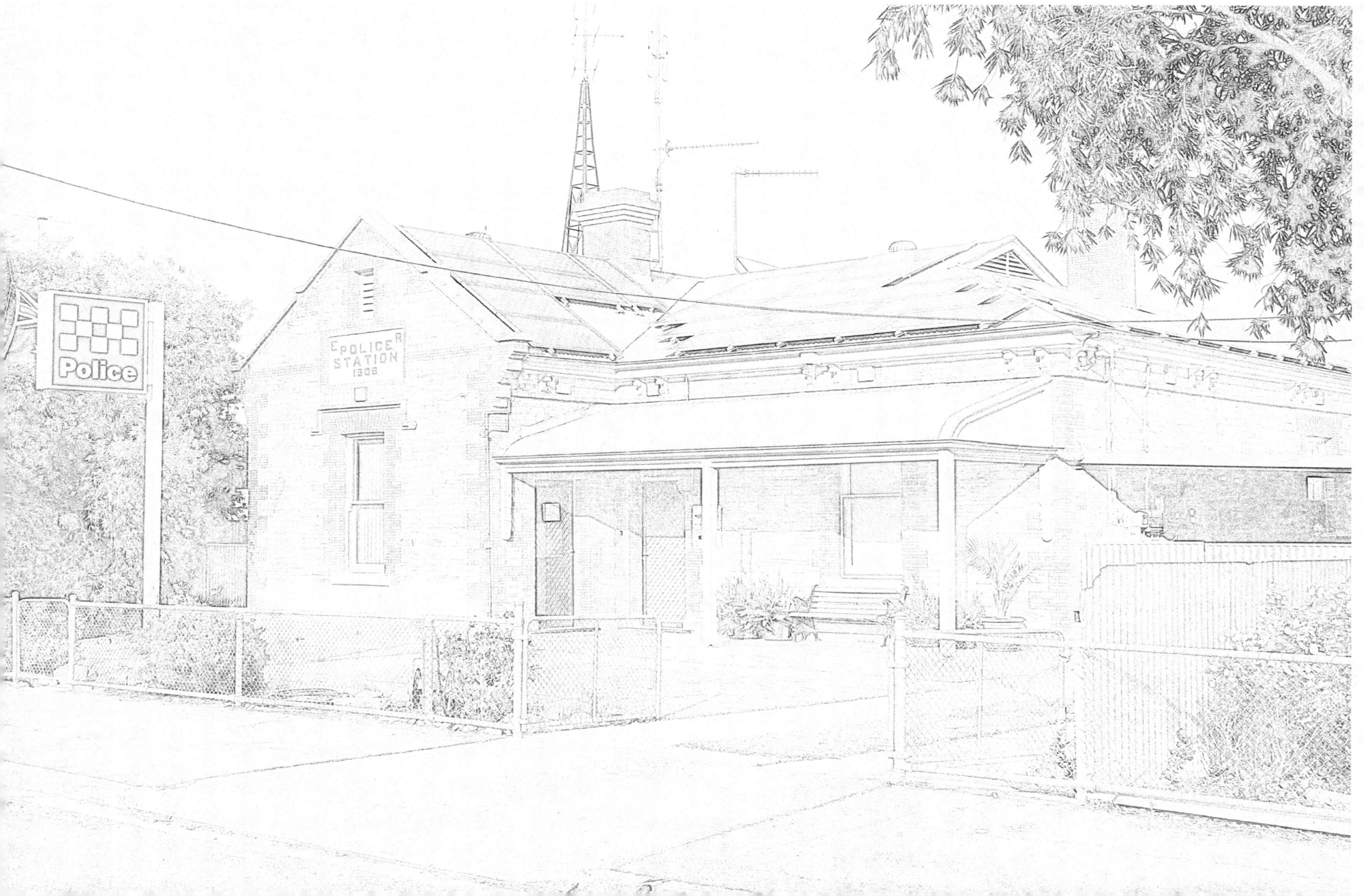
Police
E POLICE R
STATION
1906

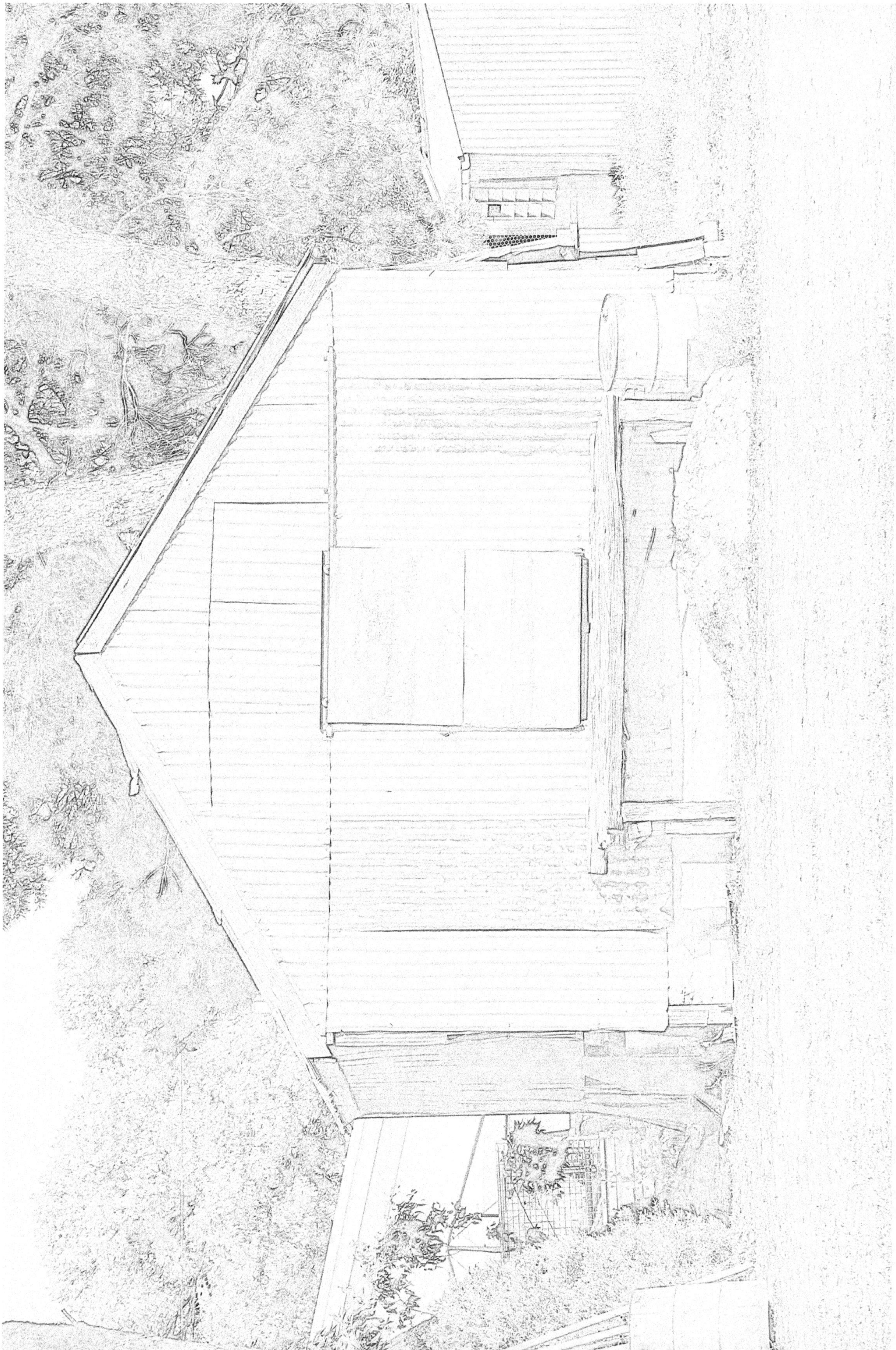

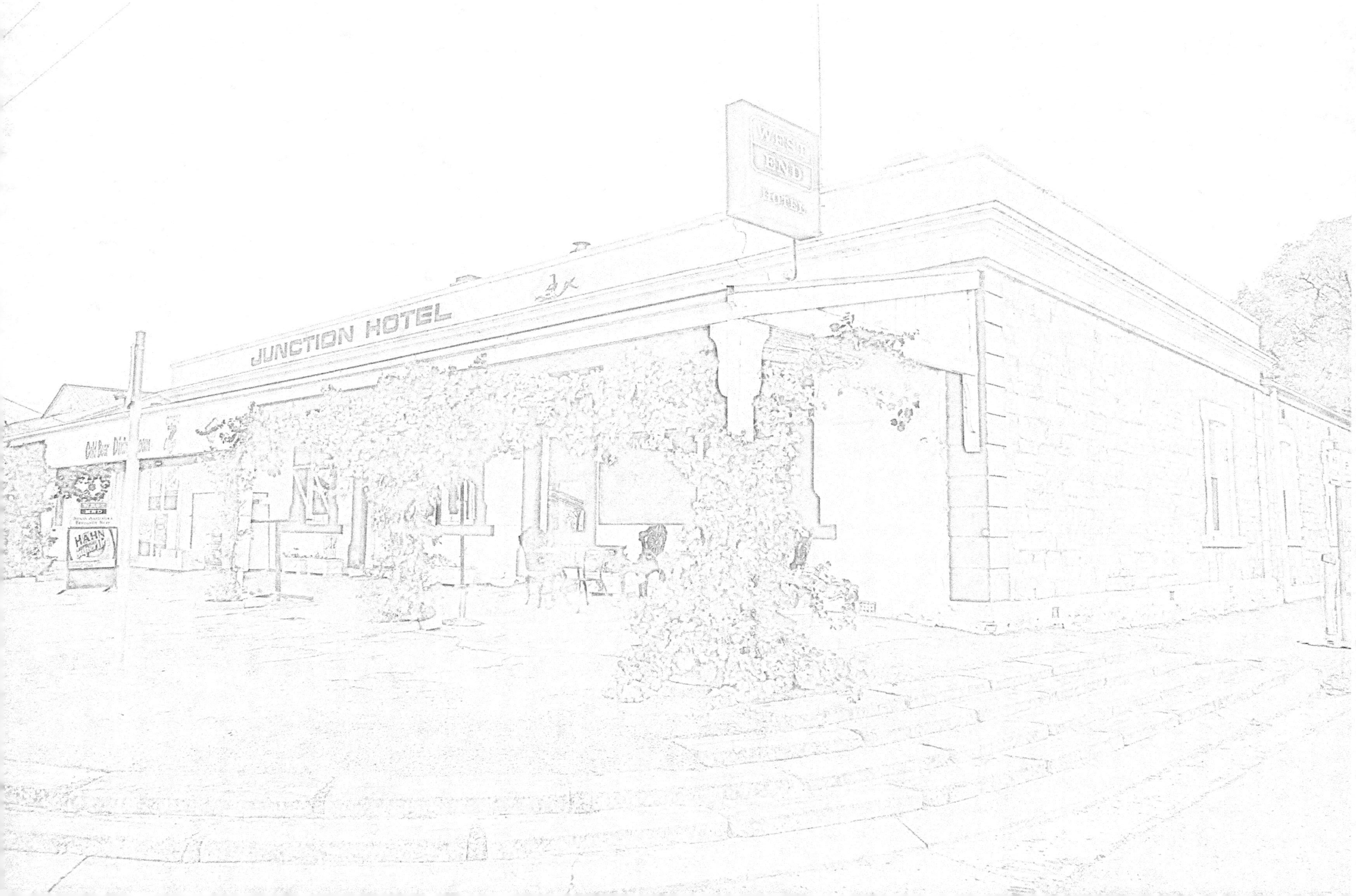
JUNCTION HOTEL
WEST END
HAHN

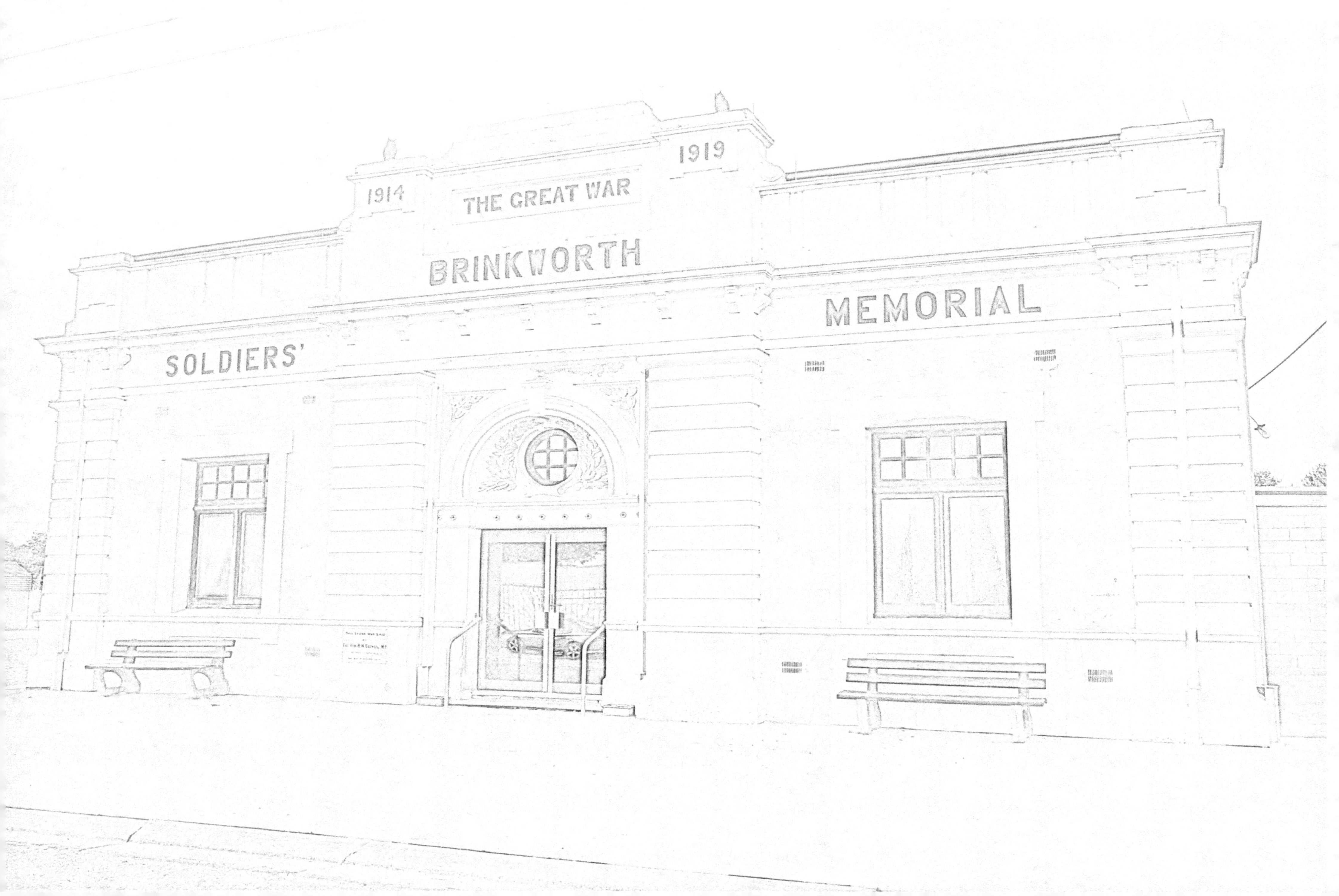
1914
1919
THE GREAT WAR
BRINKWORTH
SOLDIERS'
MEMORIAL

Butcher
DAILY KILLED MEAT
Contract Killing

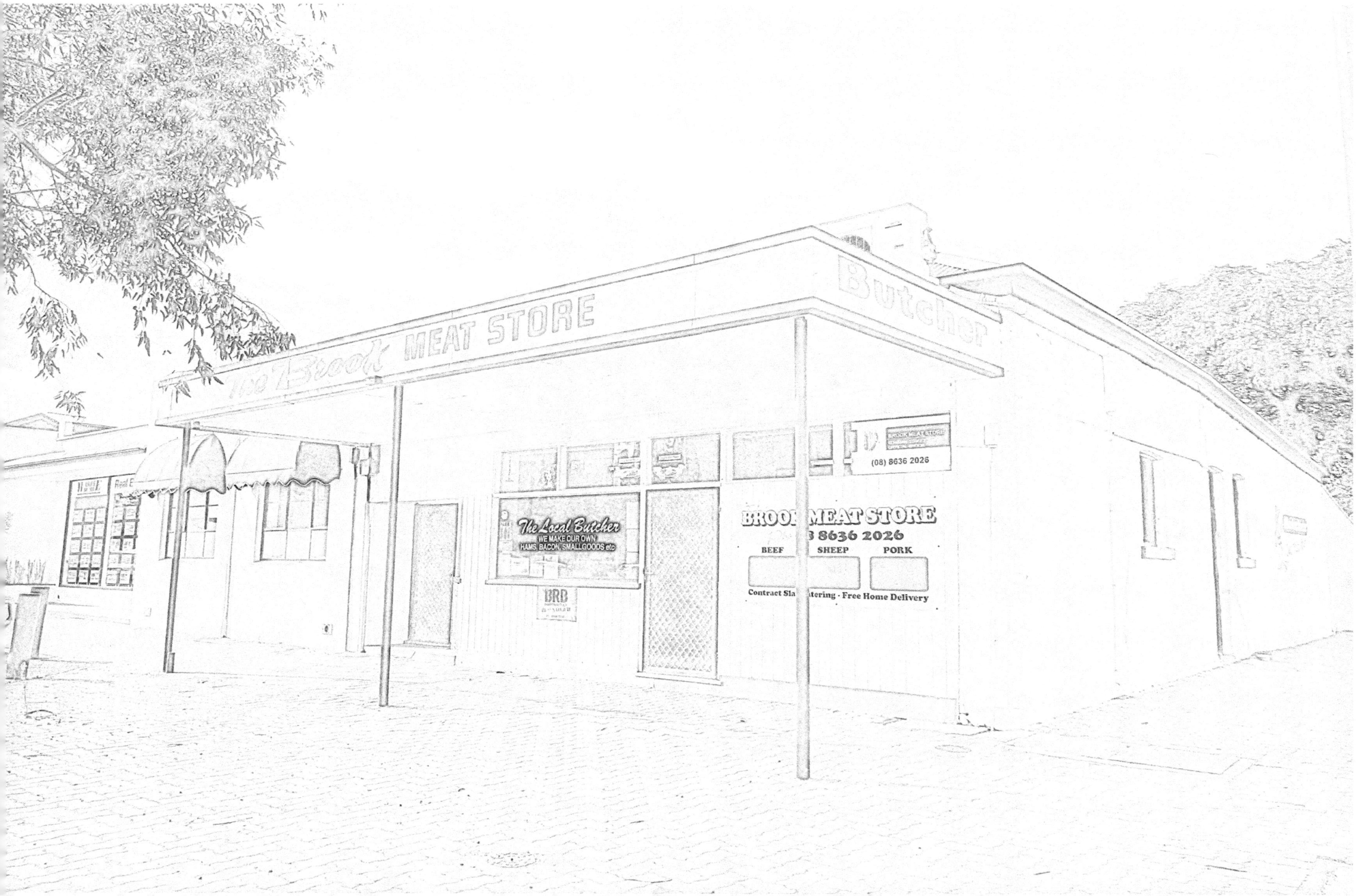

MEAT STORE
Butcher
The Local Butcher
WE MAKE OUR OWN
HAMS, BACON, SMALLGOODS etc
(08) 8636 2026
BEEF
SHEEP
PORK
BRB

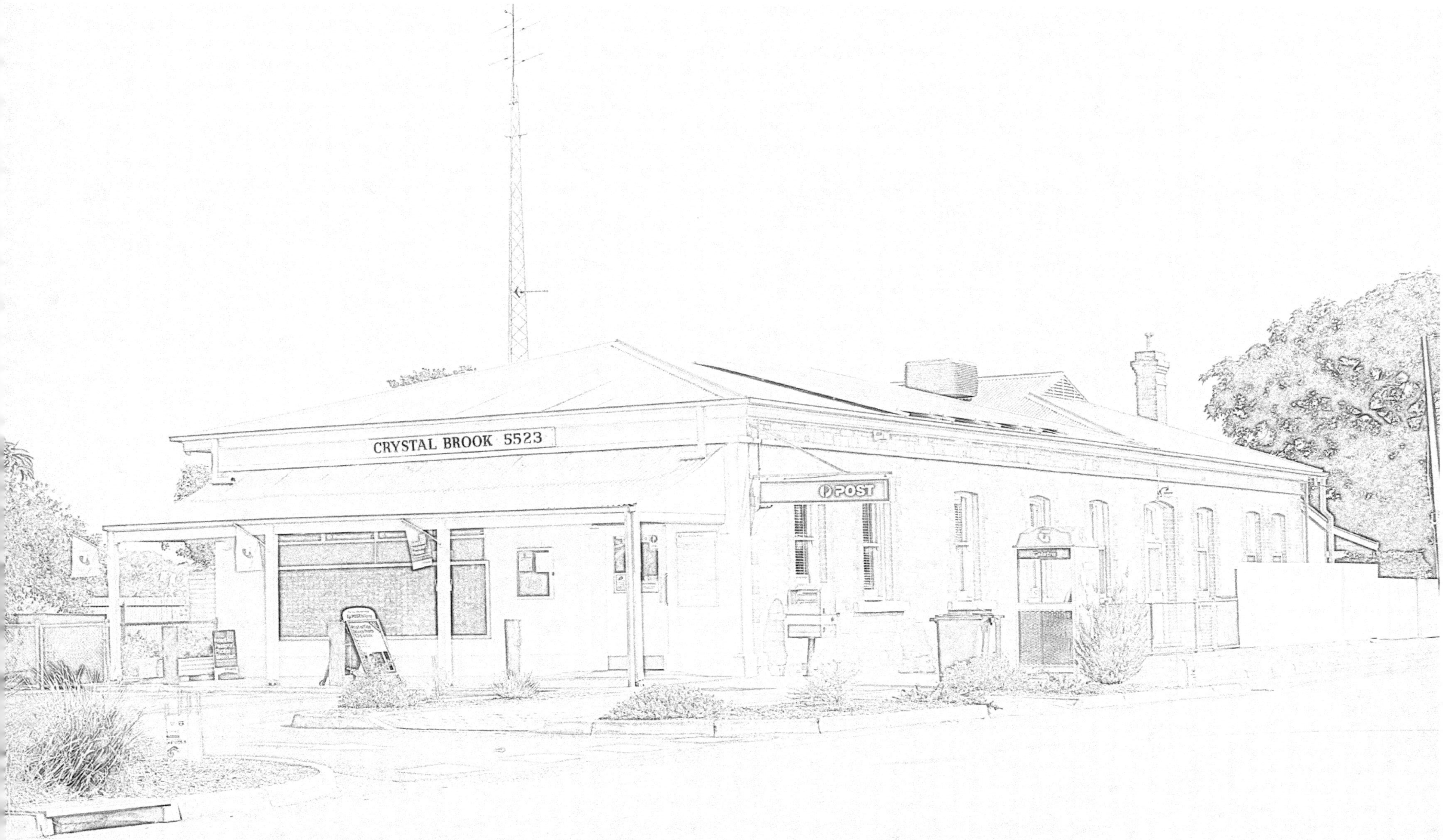
CRYSTAL BROOK 5523
POST

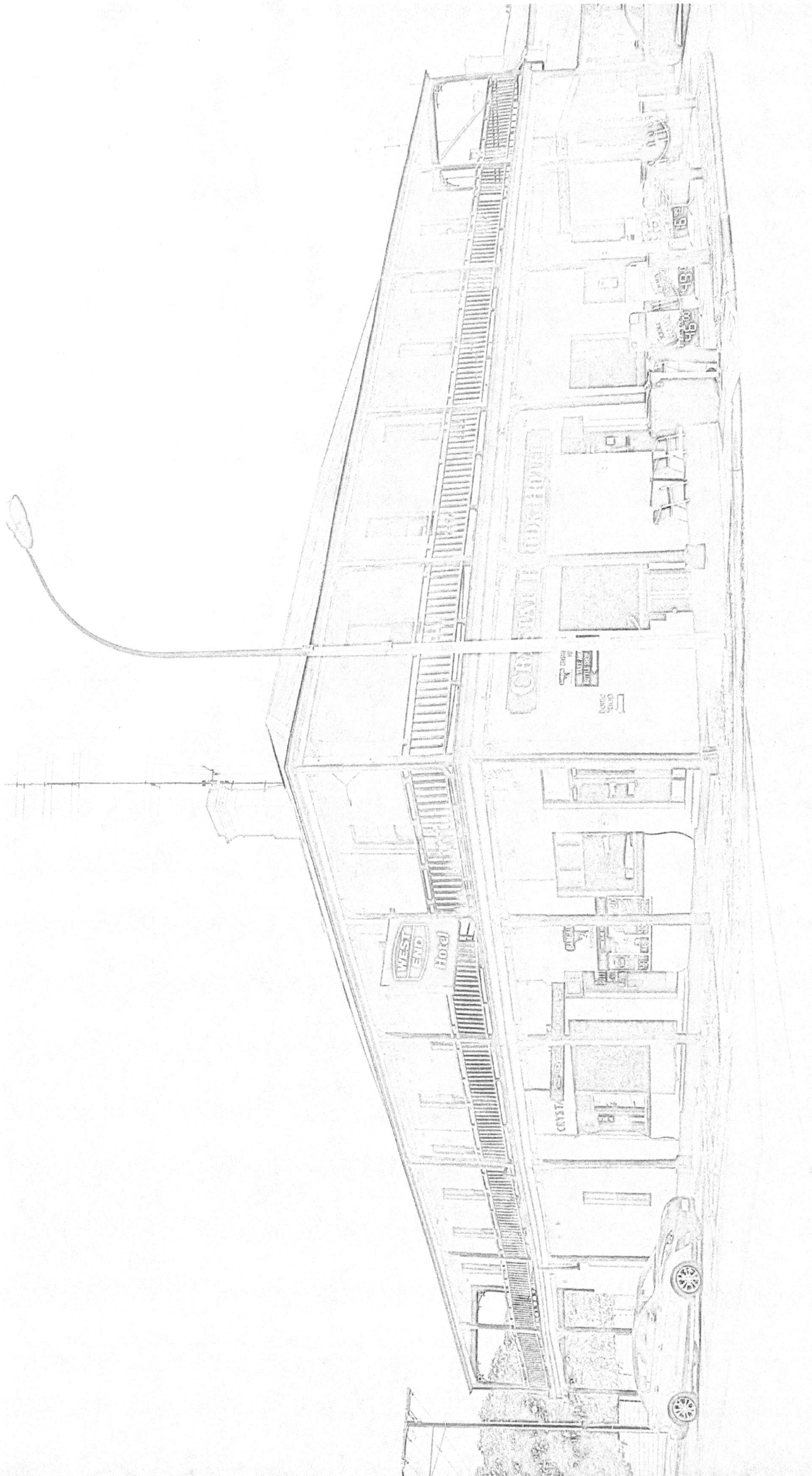
WEST END
Hotel

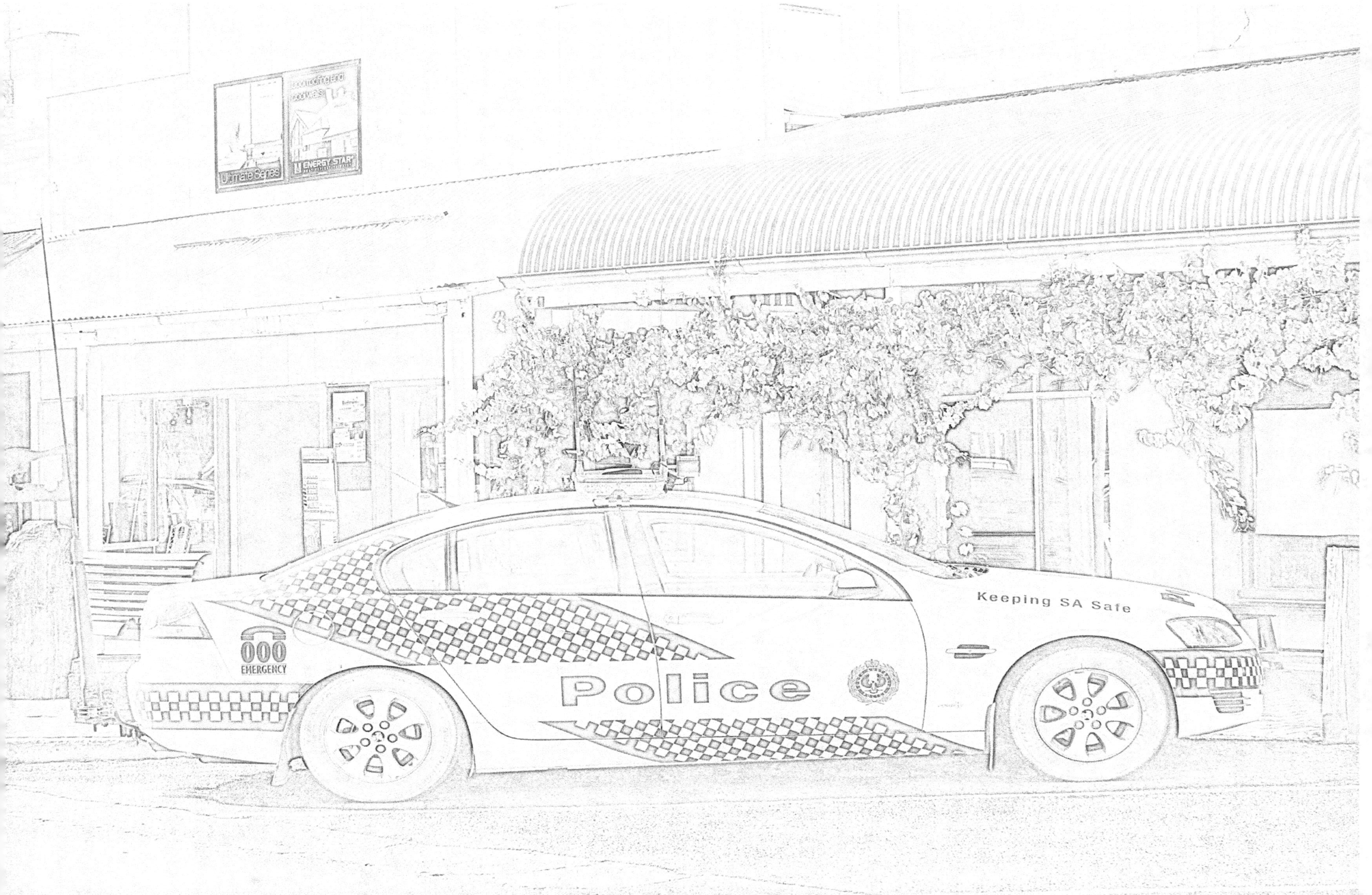
Ultimate Series
ENERGY STAR
000
EMERGENCY
Police
Keeping SA Safe

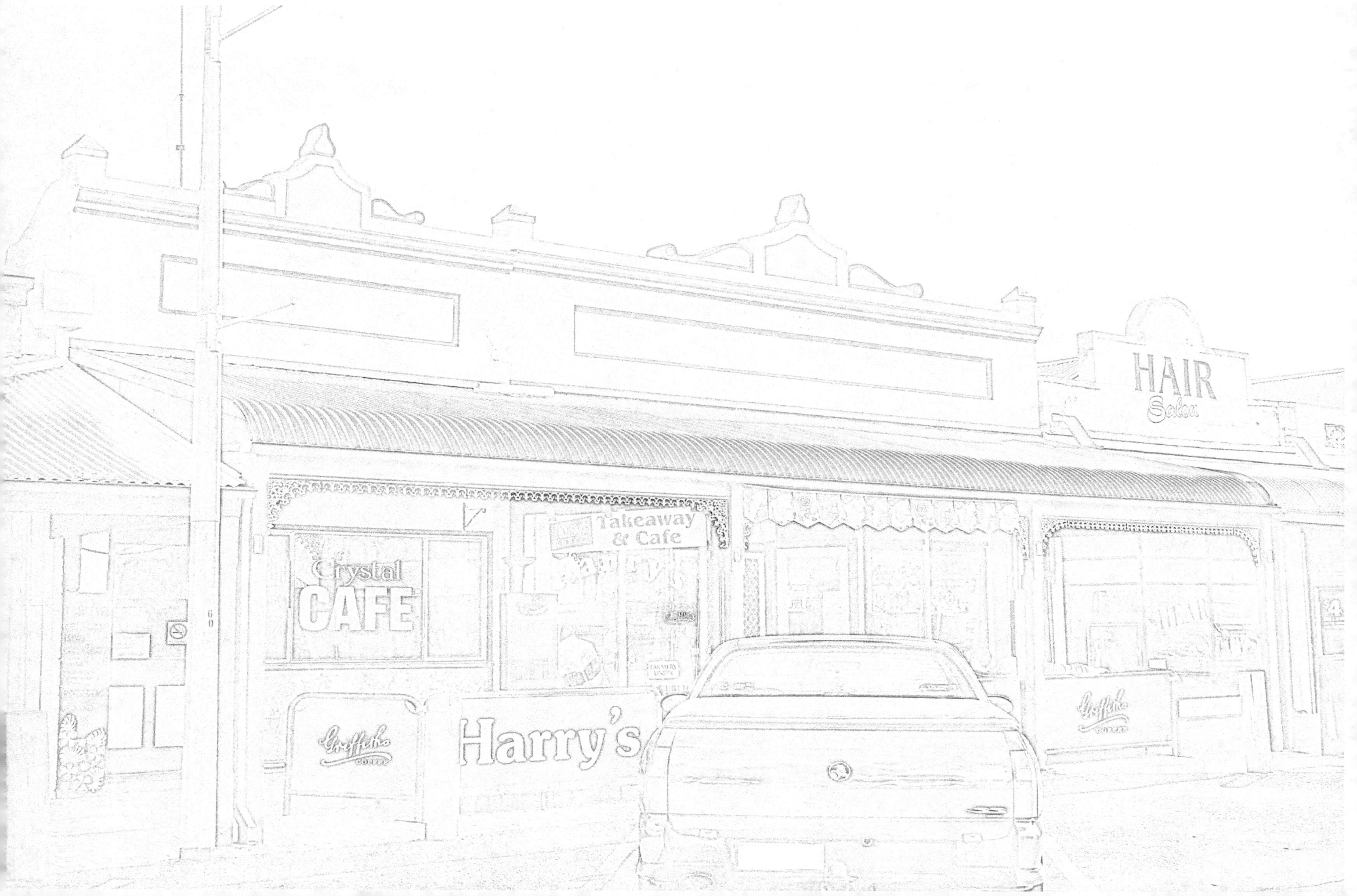
HAIR
Salon
Takeaway
& Cafe
Crystal
CAFE
Harry's

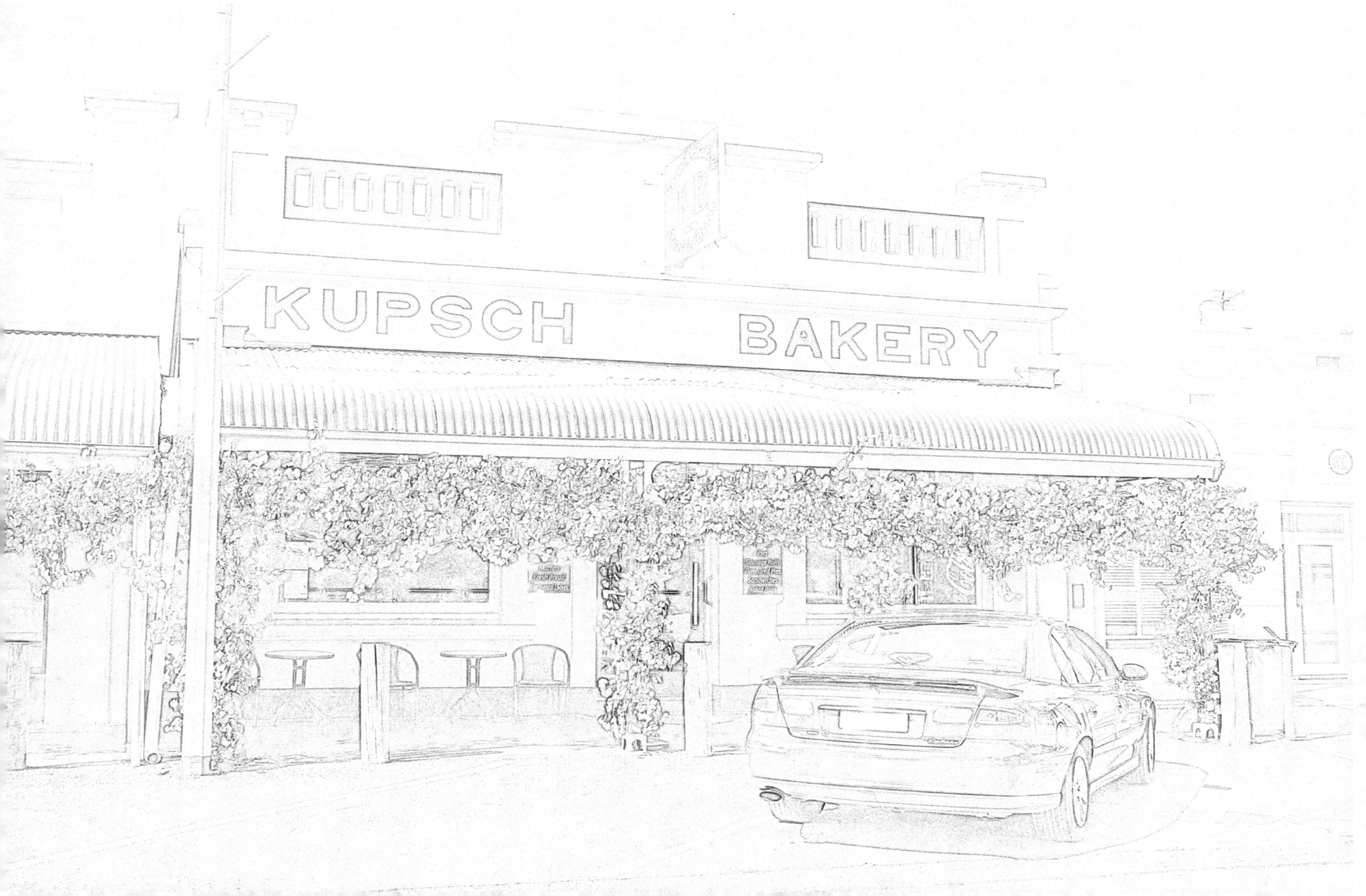
KUPSCH BAKERY

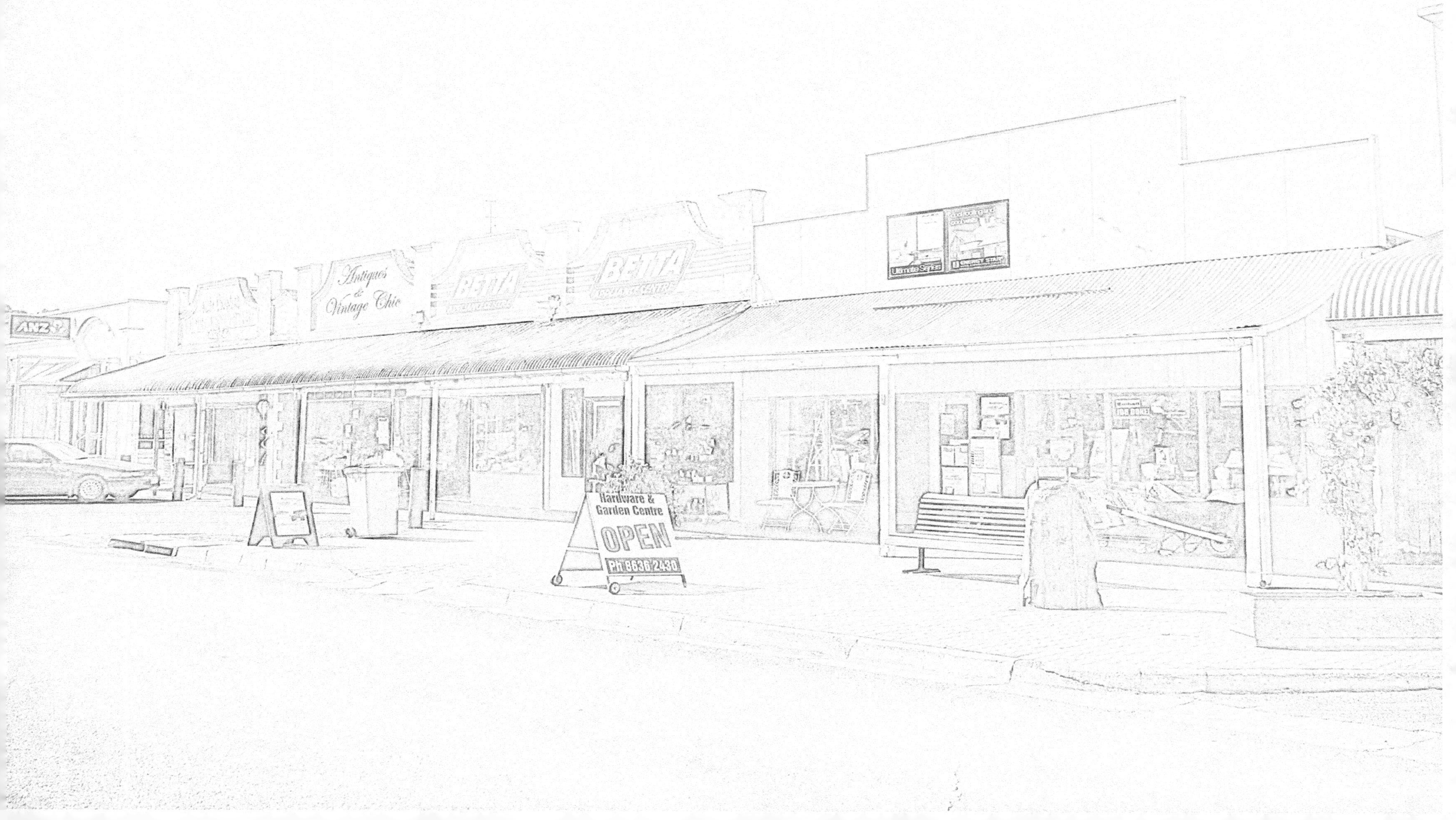
ANZ
Antiques & Vintage Chic
BETTA
BETTA
Ultimate Series
Hardware & Garden Centre
OPEN
Ph 8636 2430

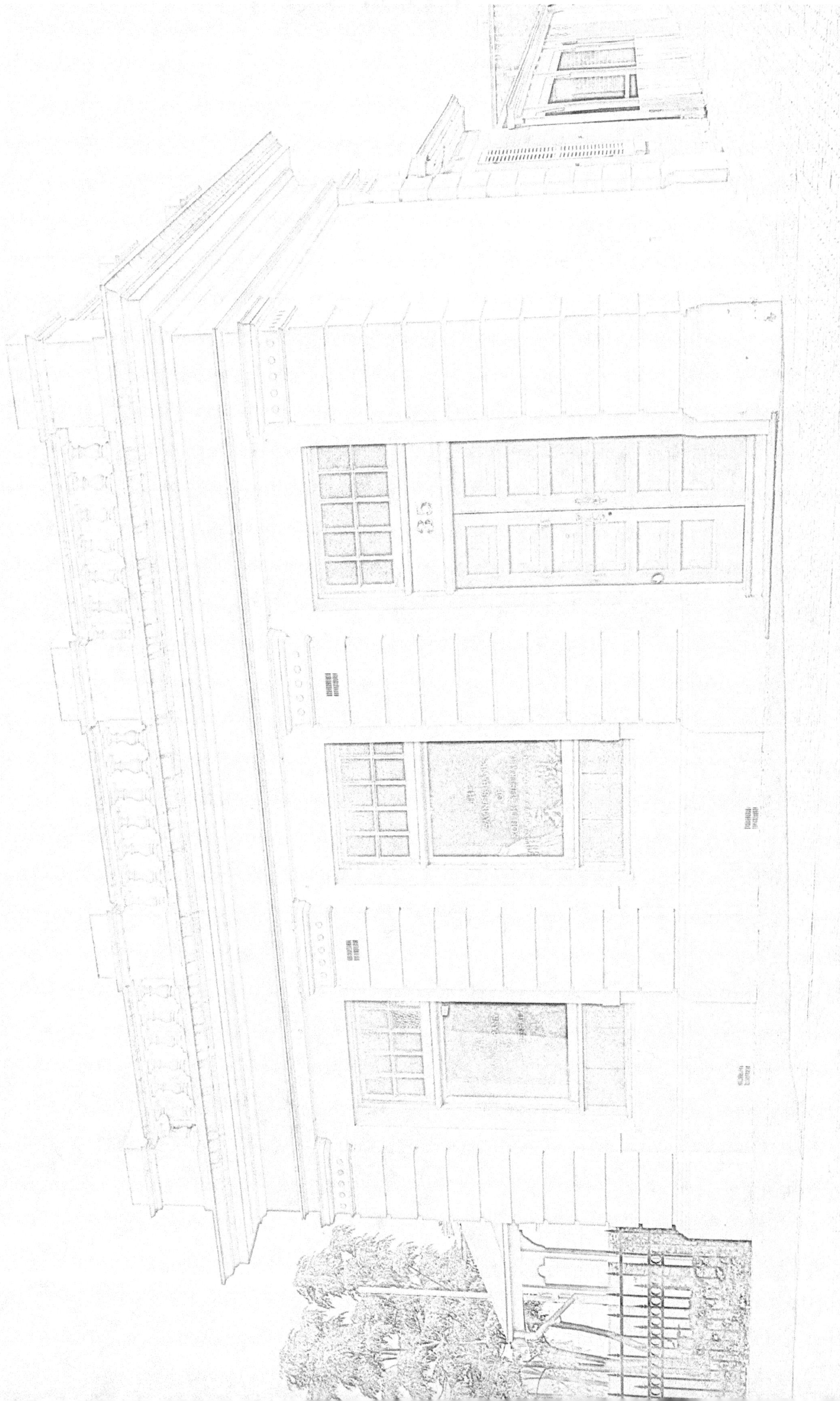

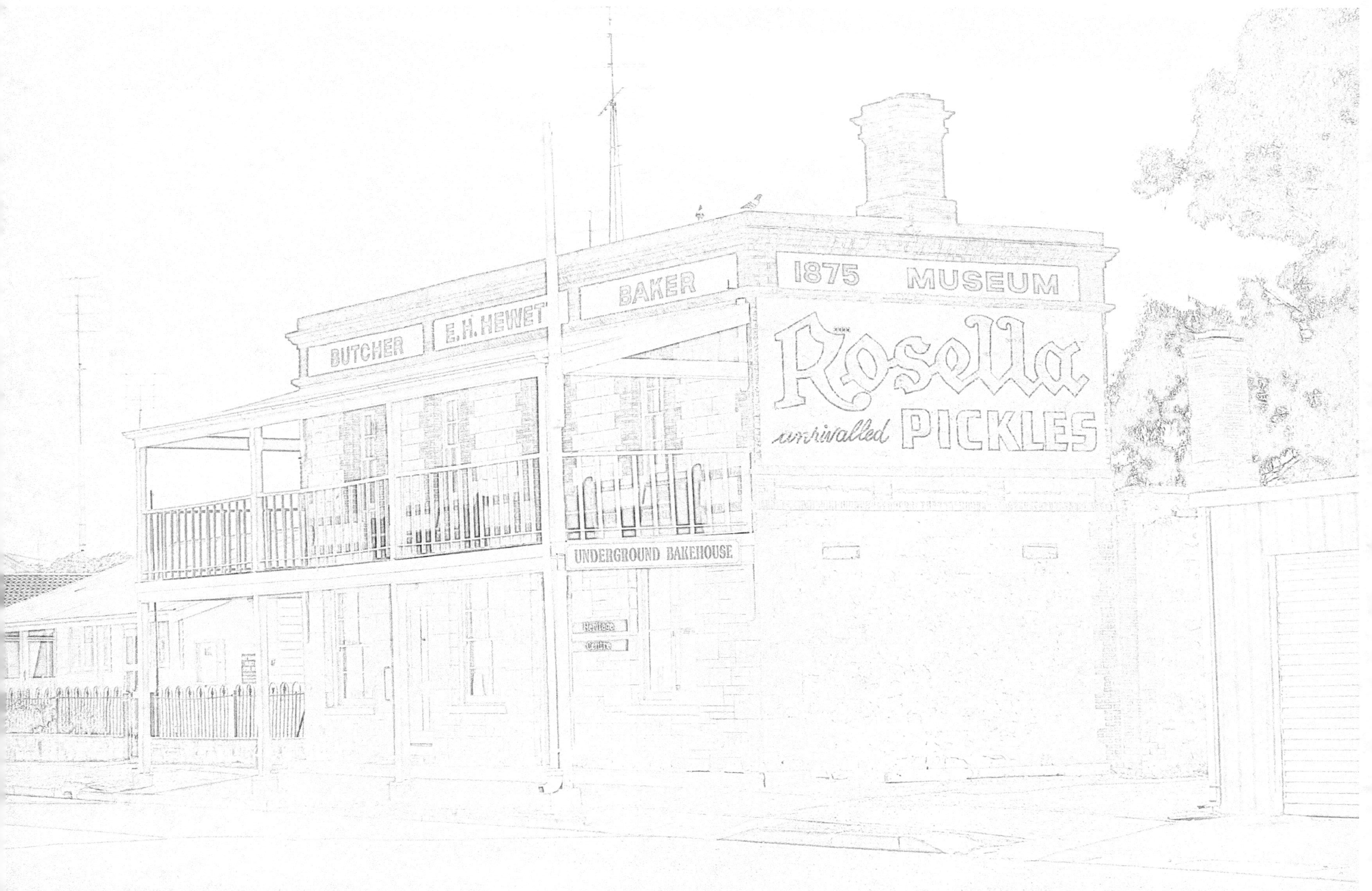

1875 MUSEUM
BAKER
E.H. HEWET
BUTCHER
Rosella
unrivalled PICKLES
UNDERGROUND BAKEHOUSE
Heritage
Centre

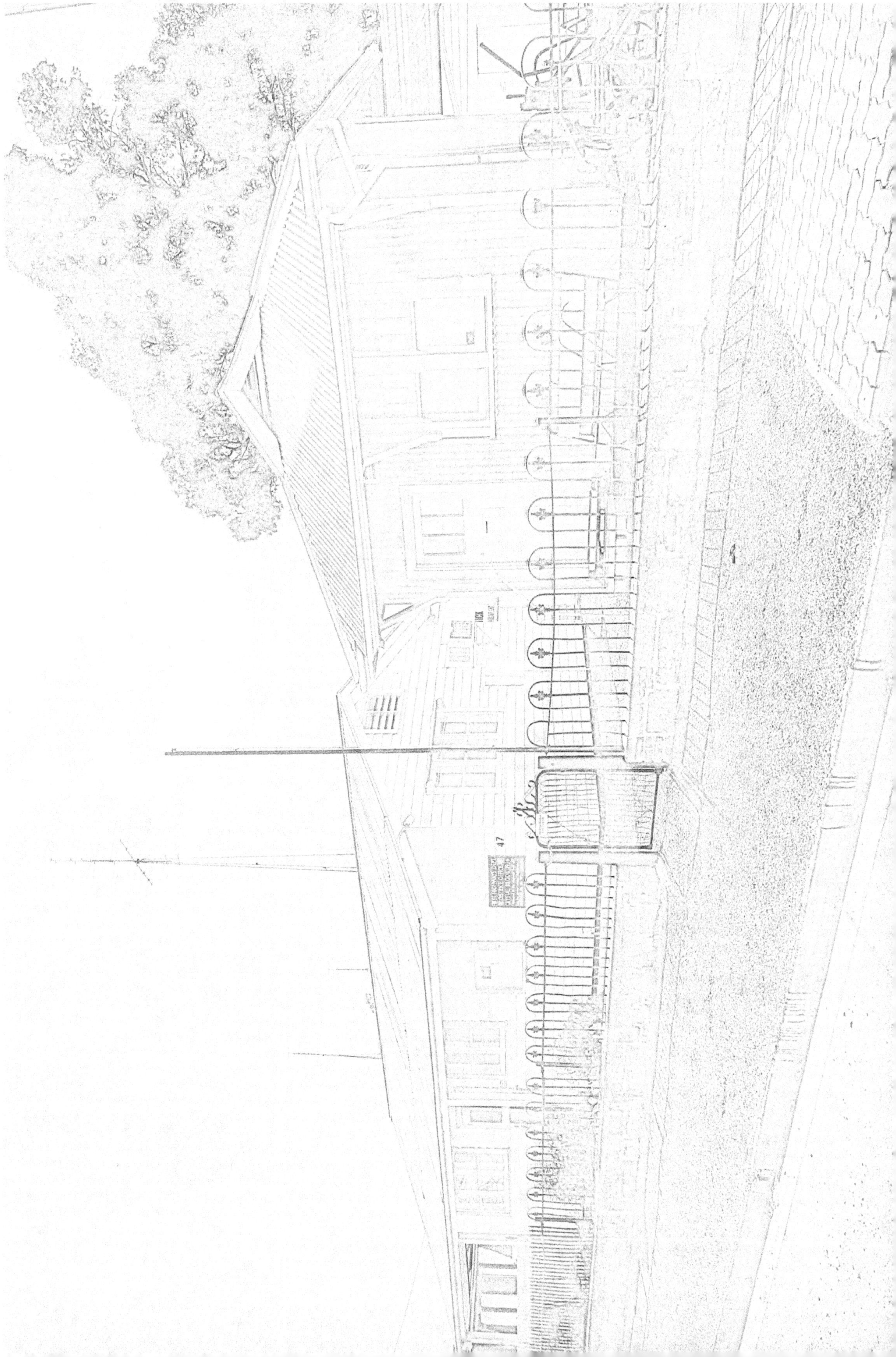

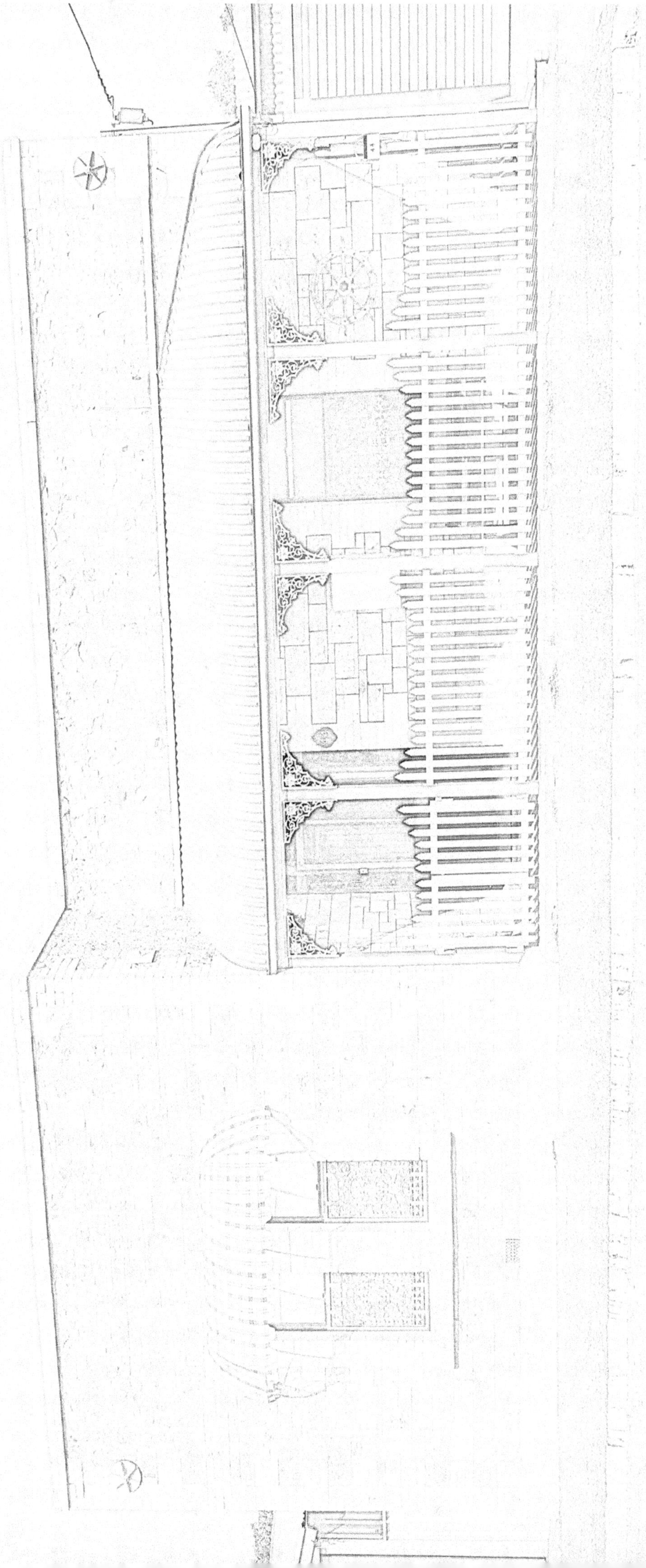

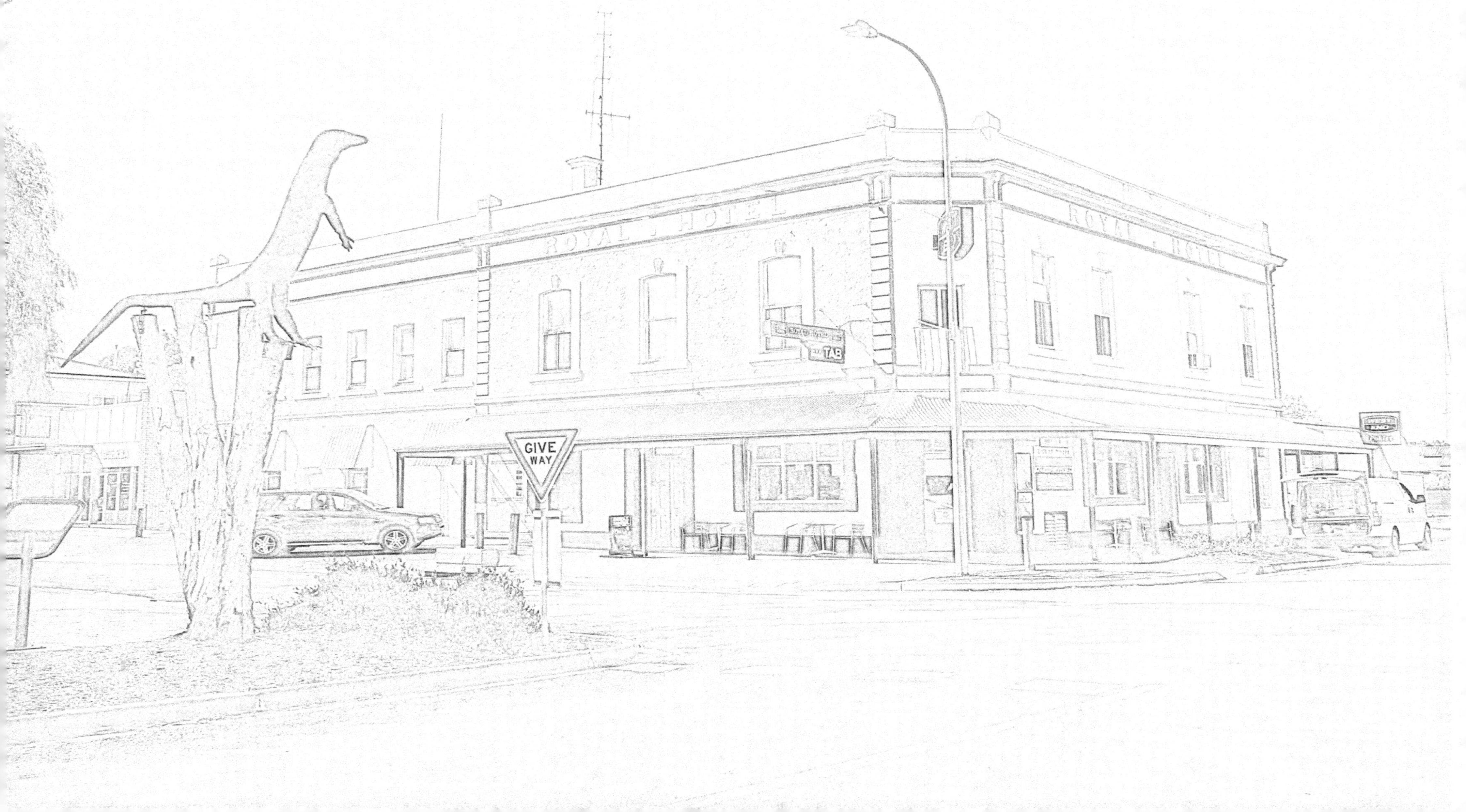
ROYAL HOTEL
TAB
ROYAL HOTEL
GIVE WAY

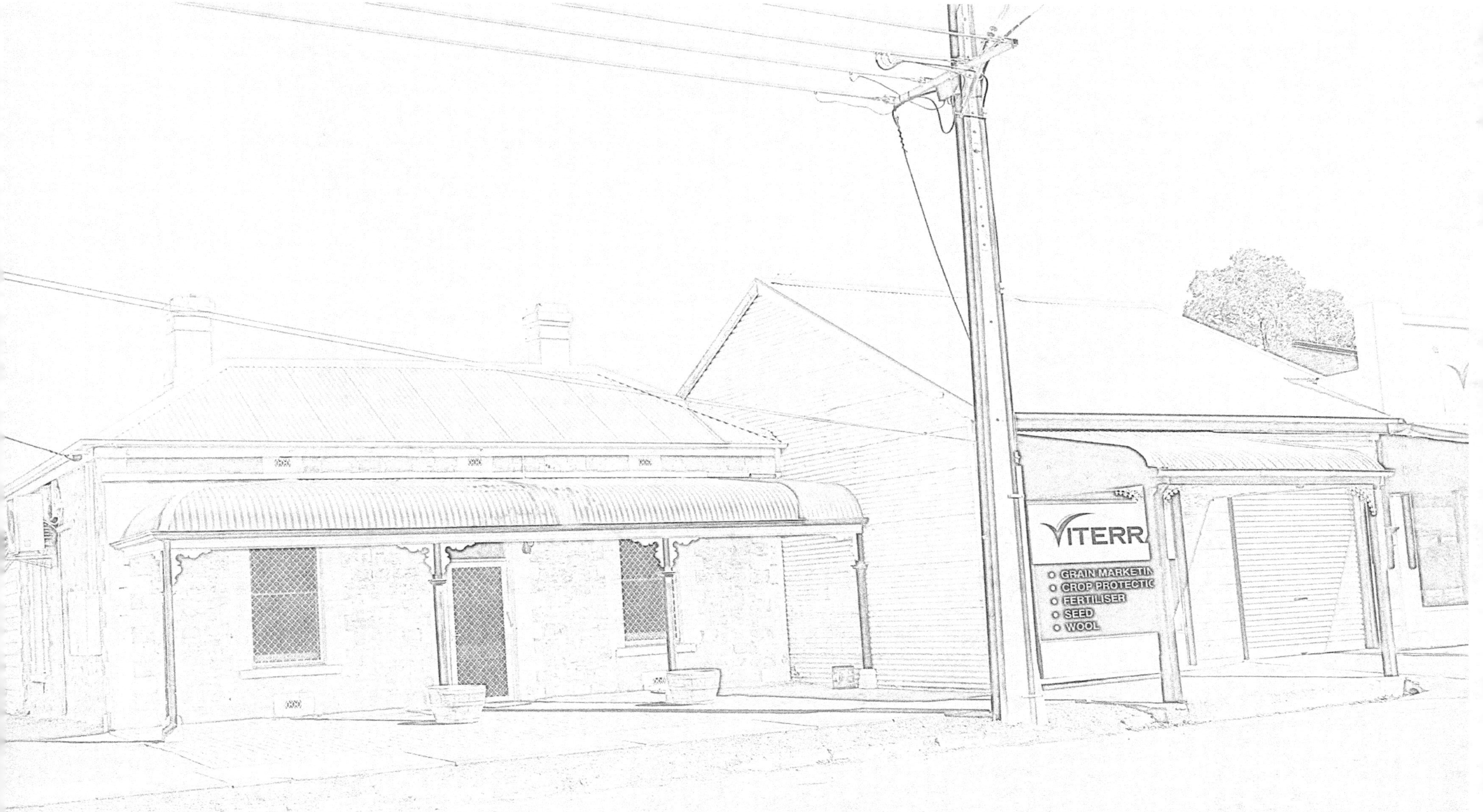
VITERR
GRAIN MARKETIN
CROP PROTECTIC
FERTILISER
SEED
WOOL

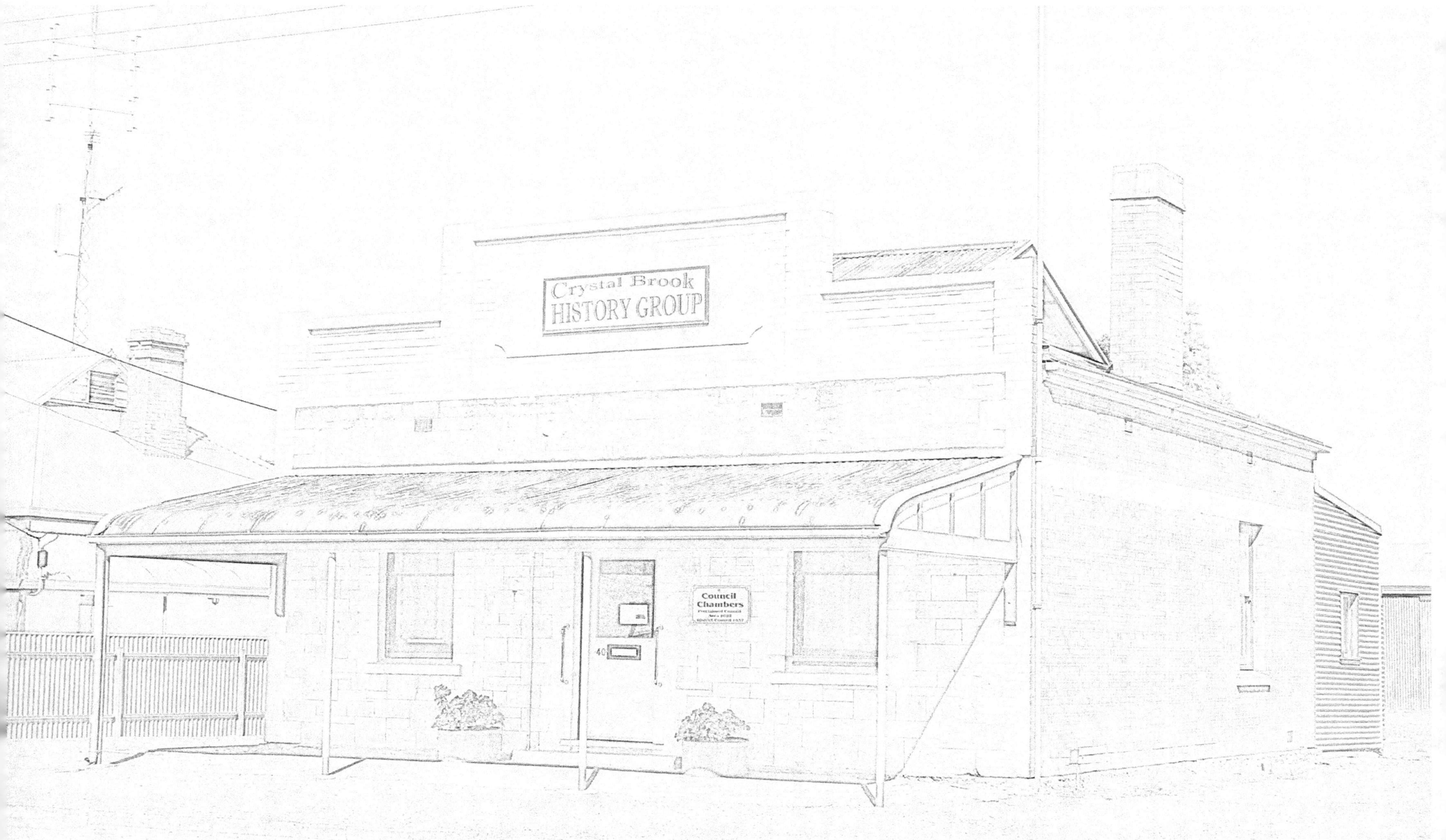
Crystal Brook
HISTORY GROUP
Council
Chambers
40

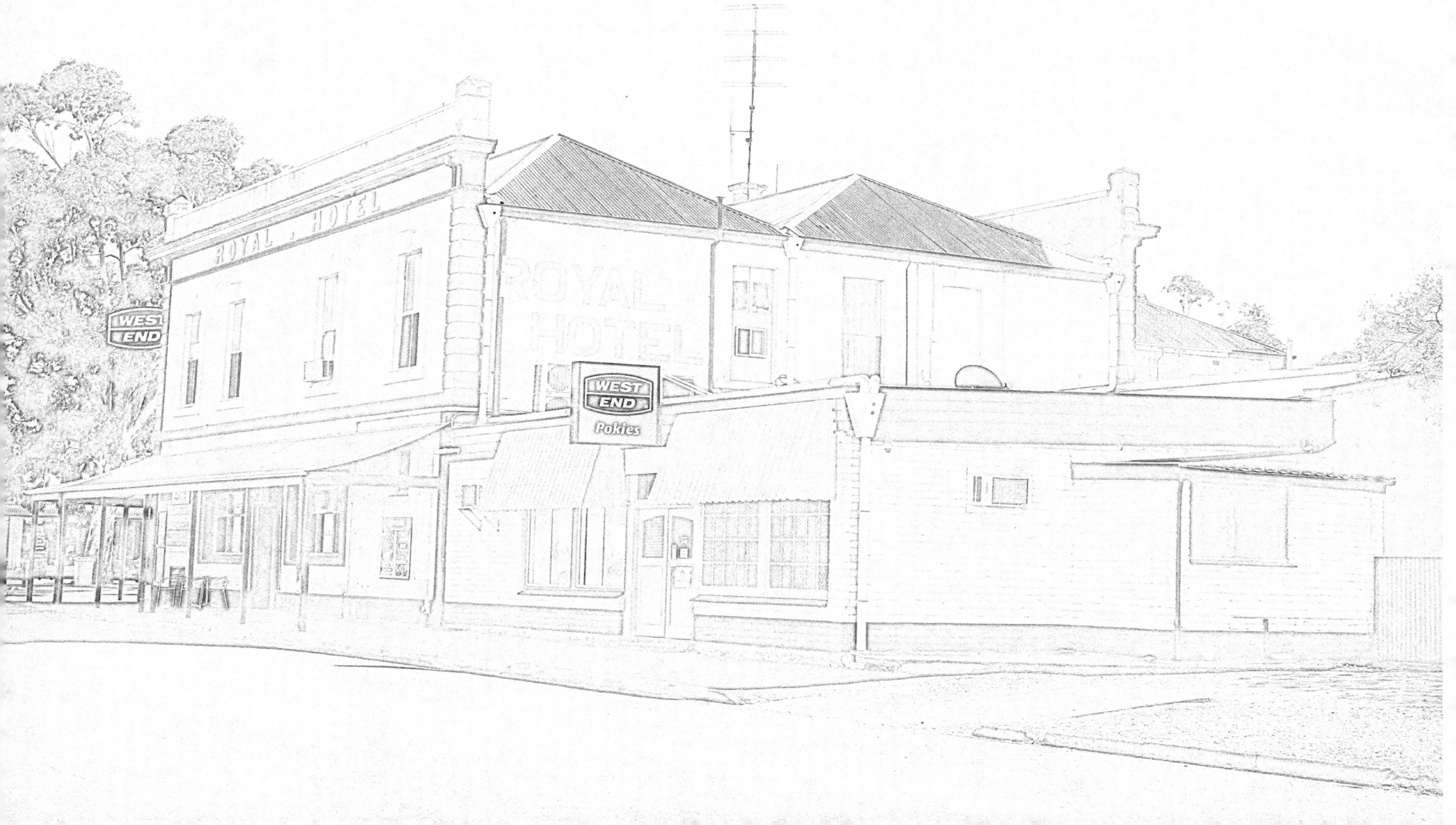
ROYAL HOTEL
WEST END
ROYAL HOTEL
WEST END
Pokies

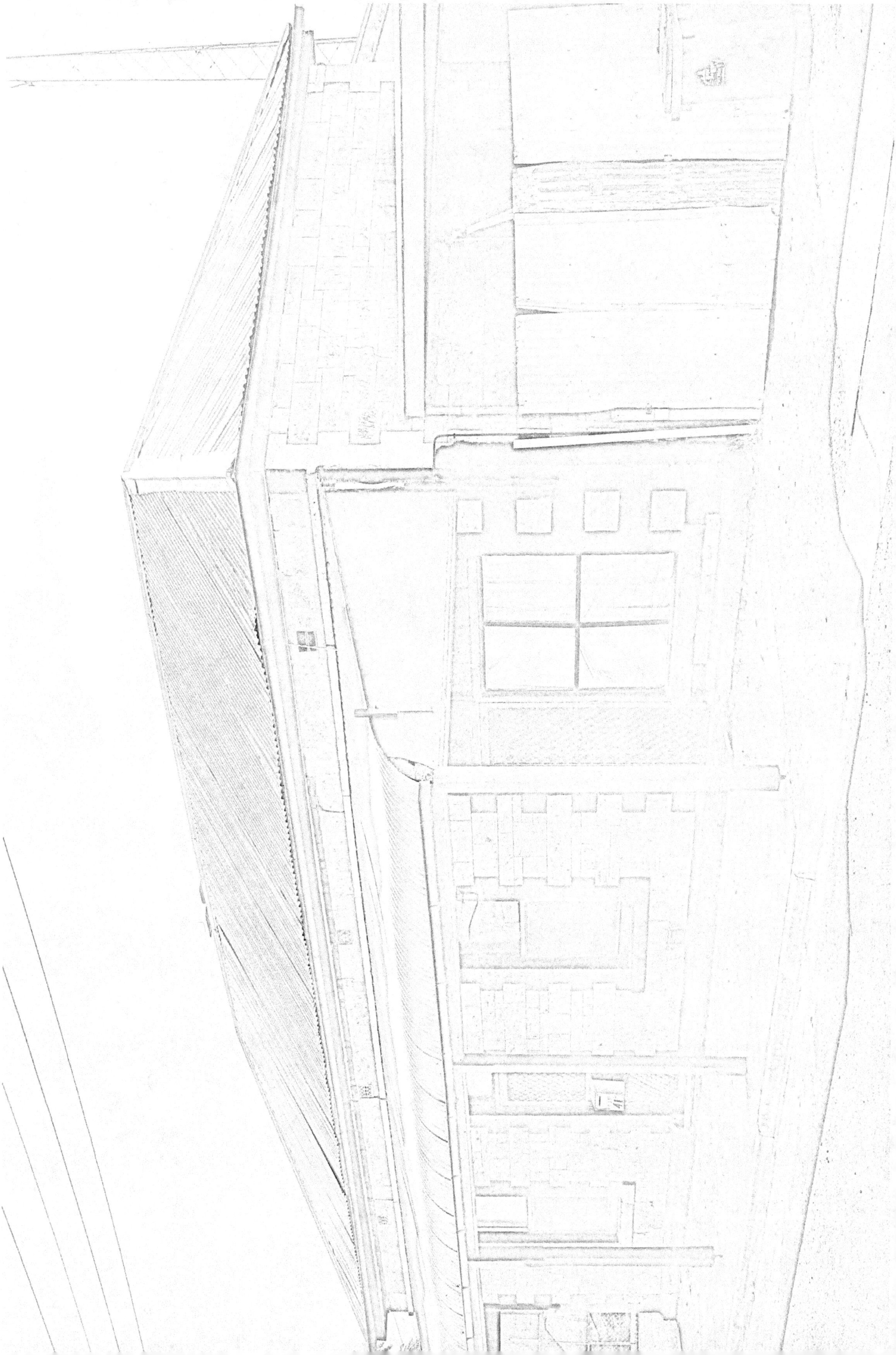

www.ingramcontent.com/pod-product-compliance
Lightning Source LLC
Chambersburg PA
CBHW081058180526
45170CB00005B/1801
* 9 7 8 0 3 5 9 9 3 5 9 2 5 *